Whimsical Bugs

A Coloring Book for All Ages

illustrated by

Rachel Jones

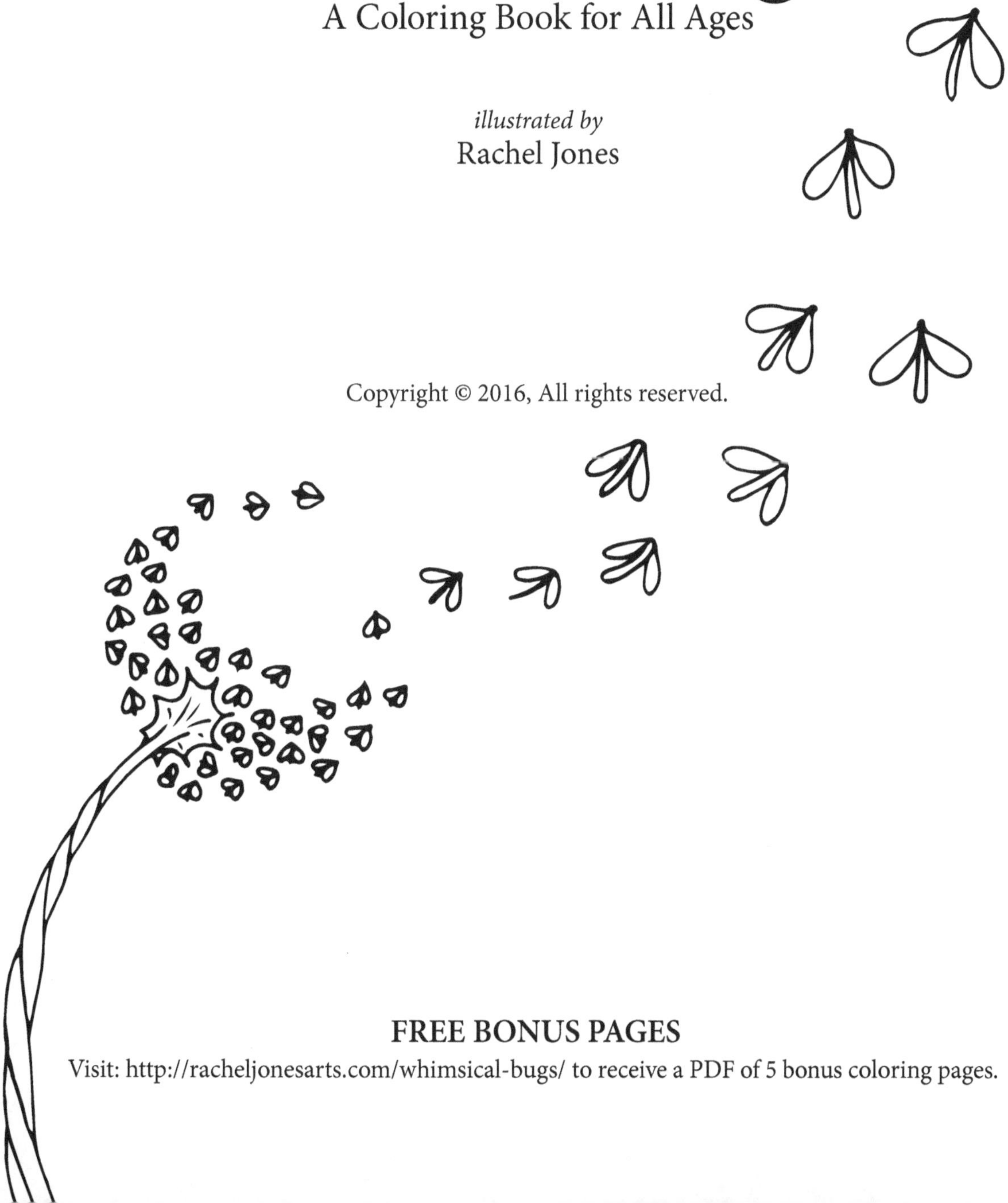

FREE BONUS PAGES

Visit: http://racheljonesarts.com/whimsical-bugs/ to receive a PDF of 5 bonus coloring pages.

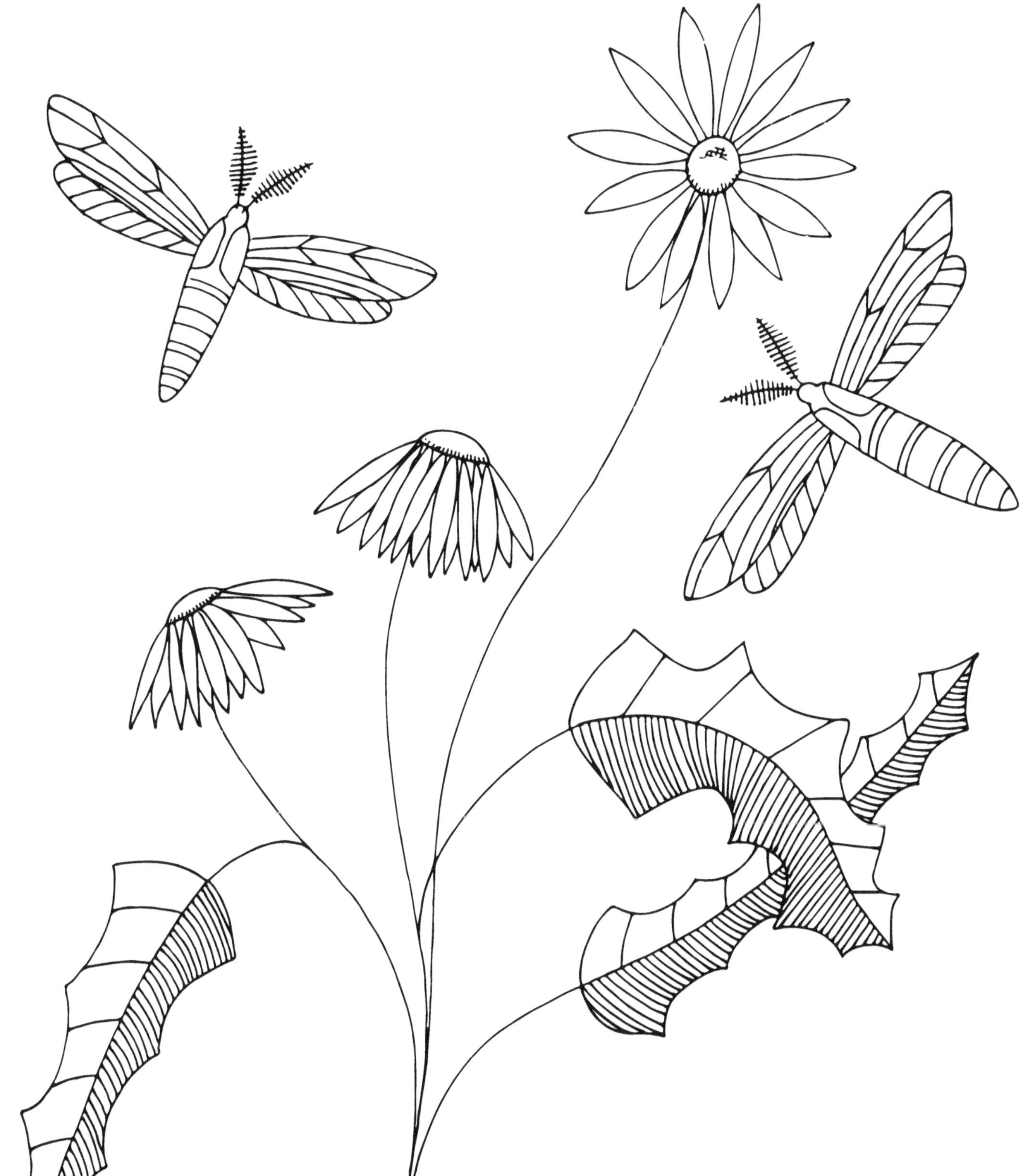

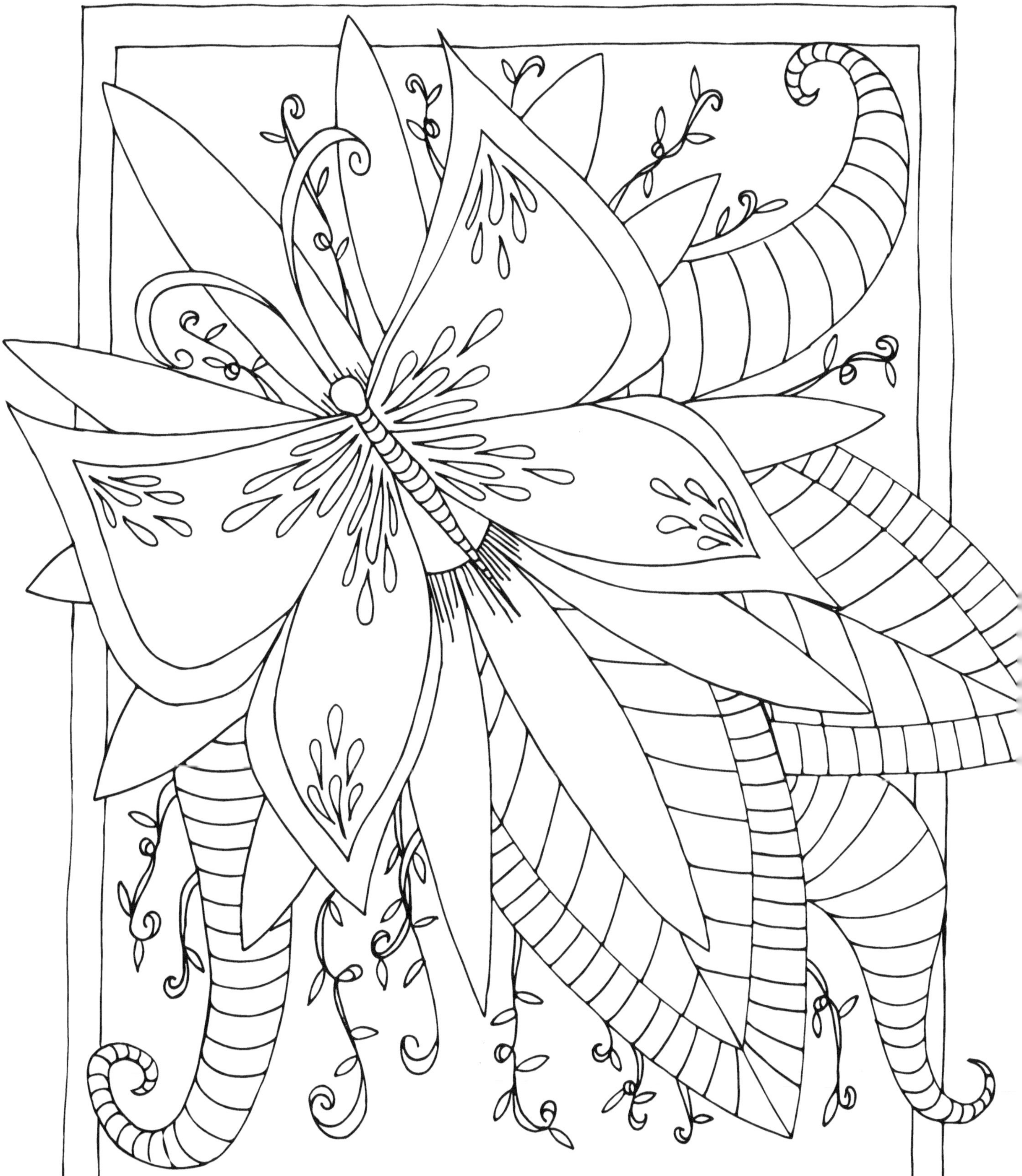

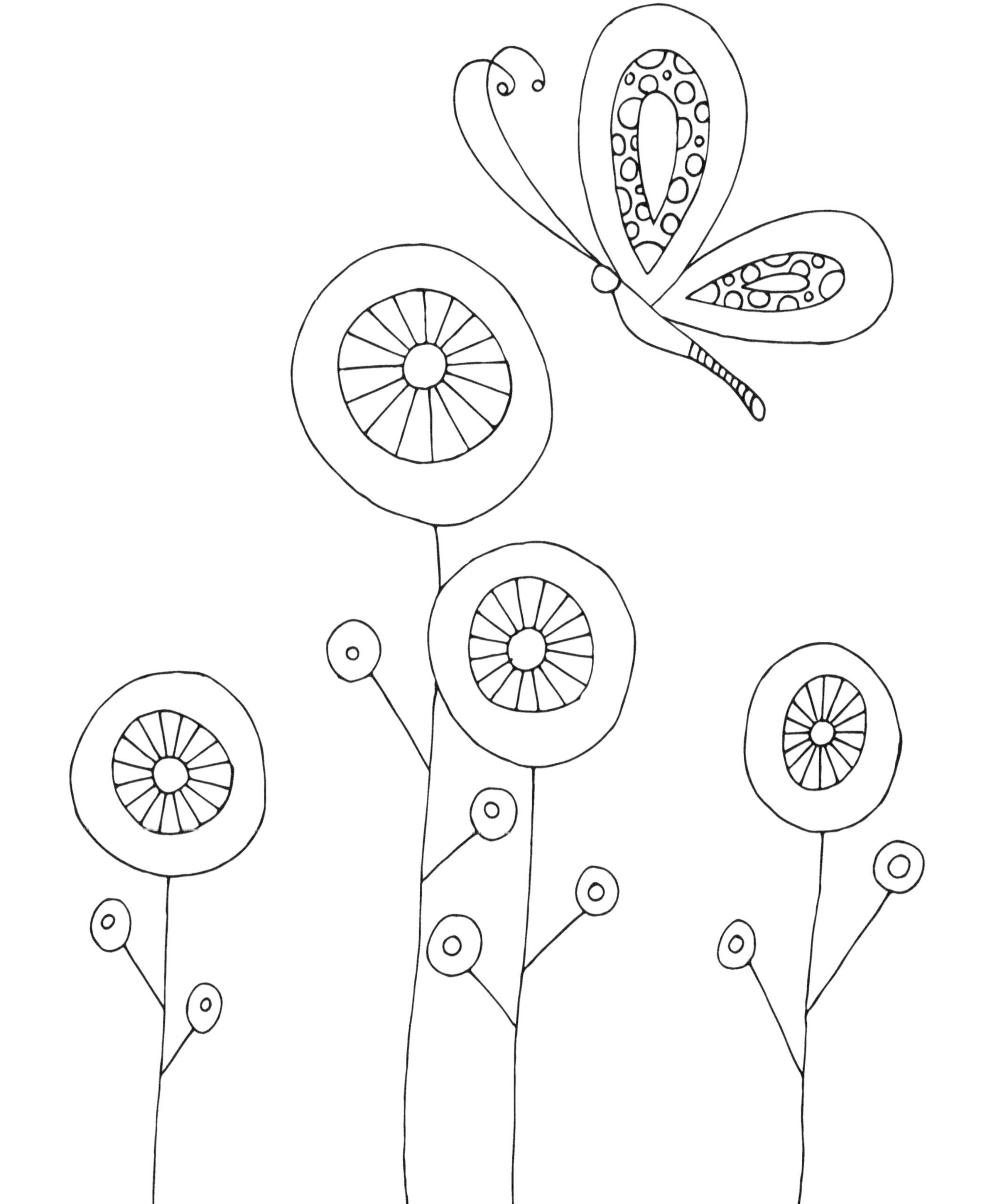

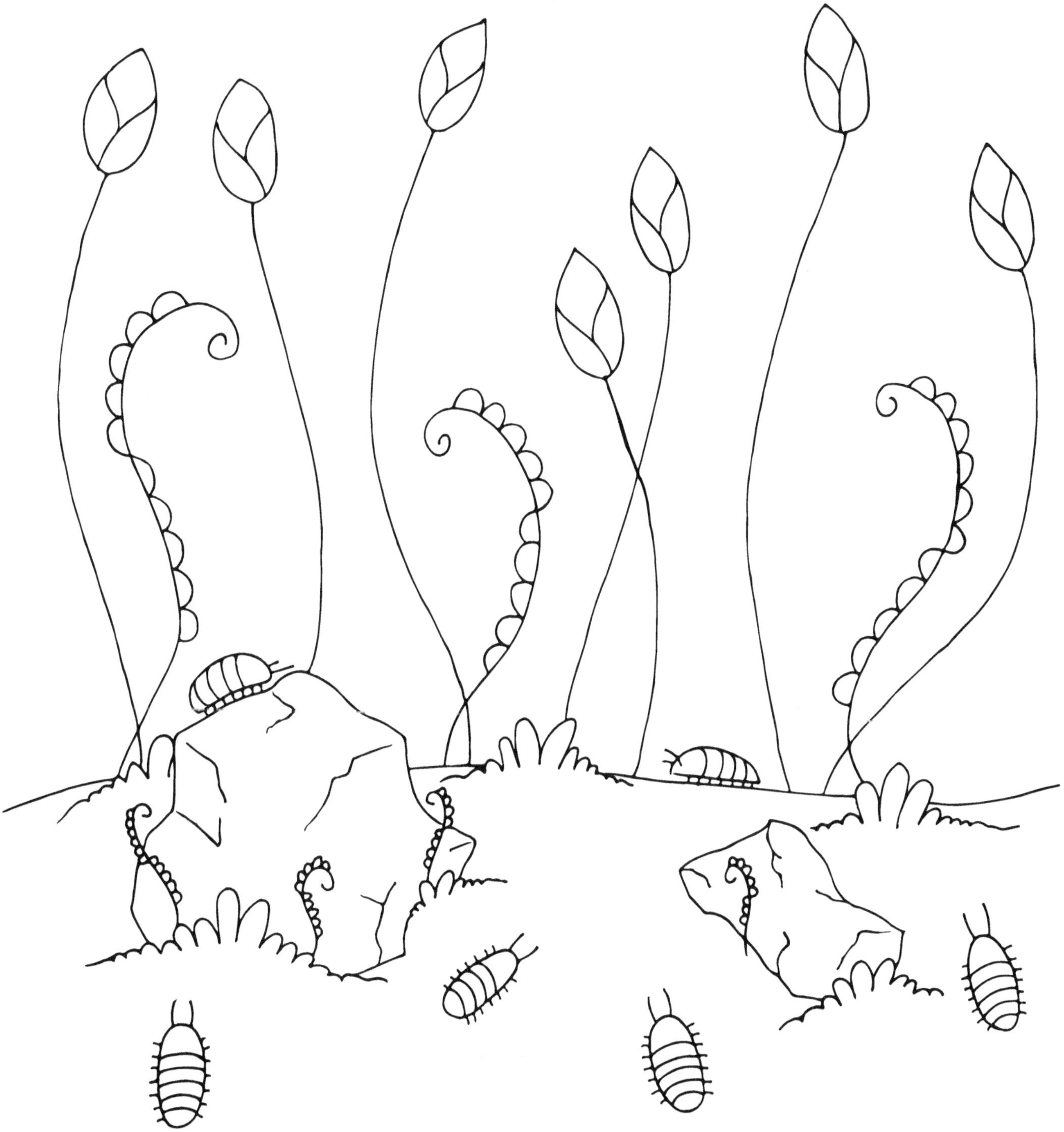

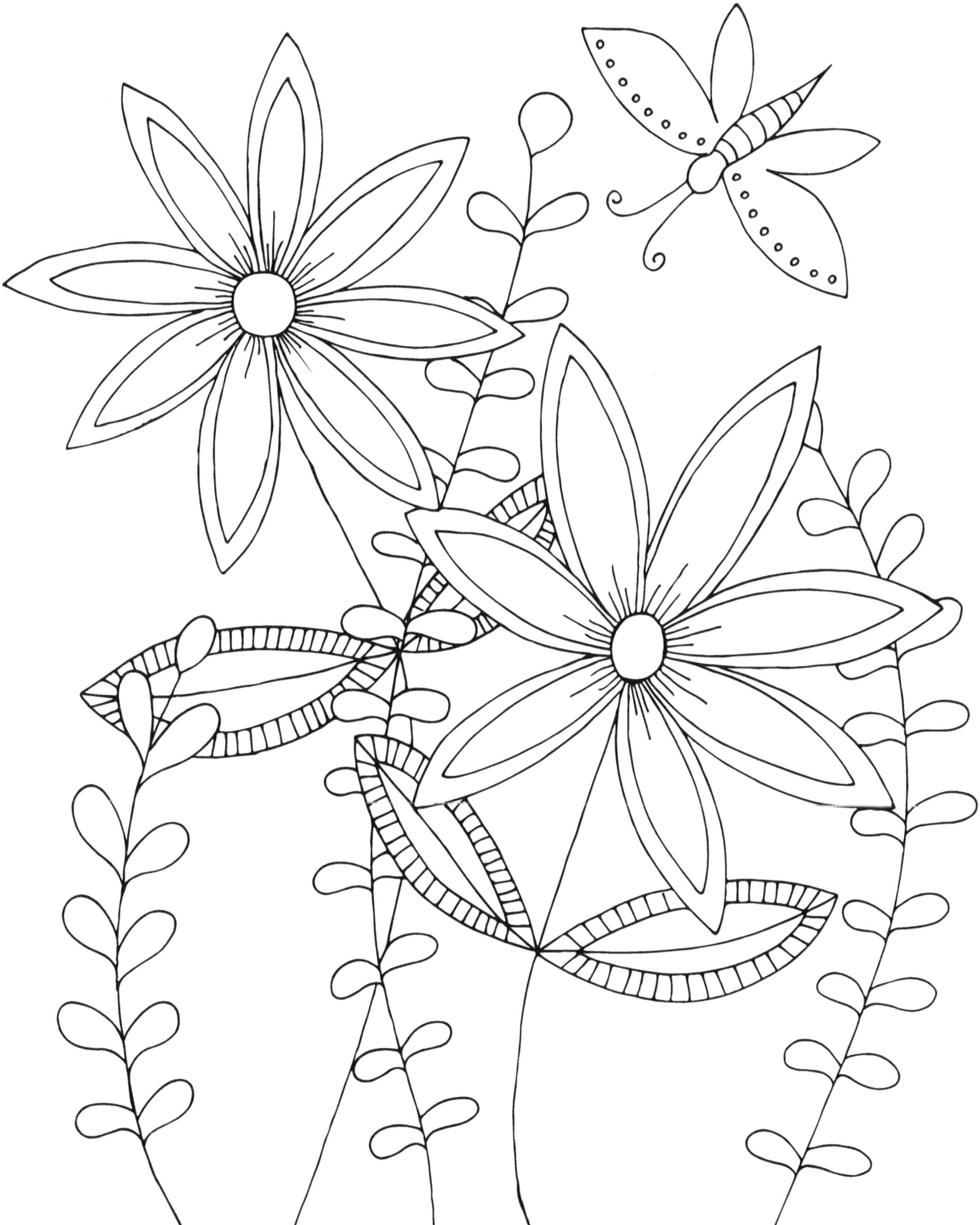

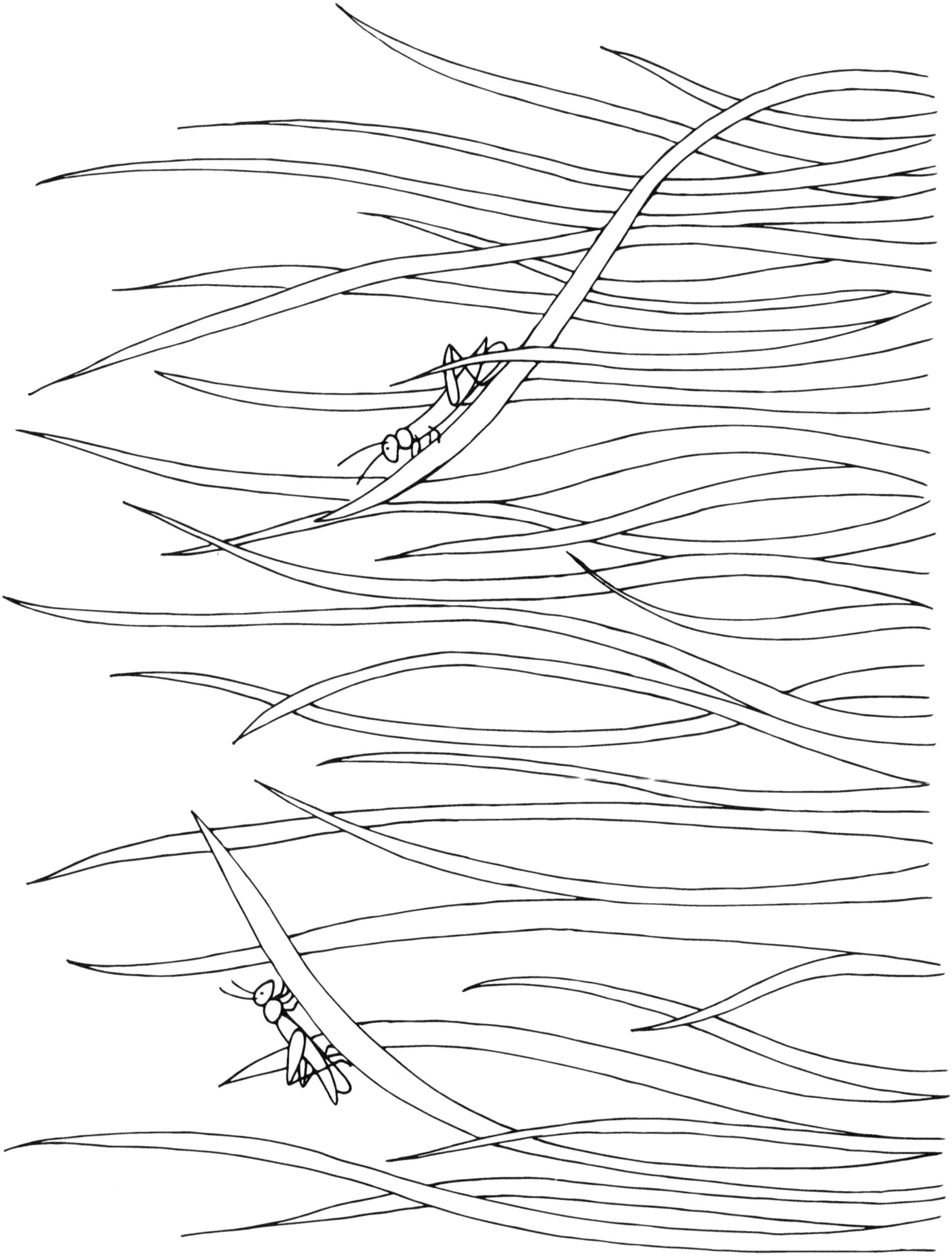

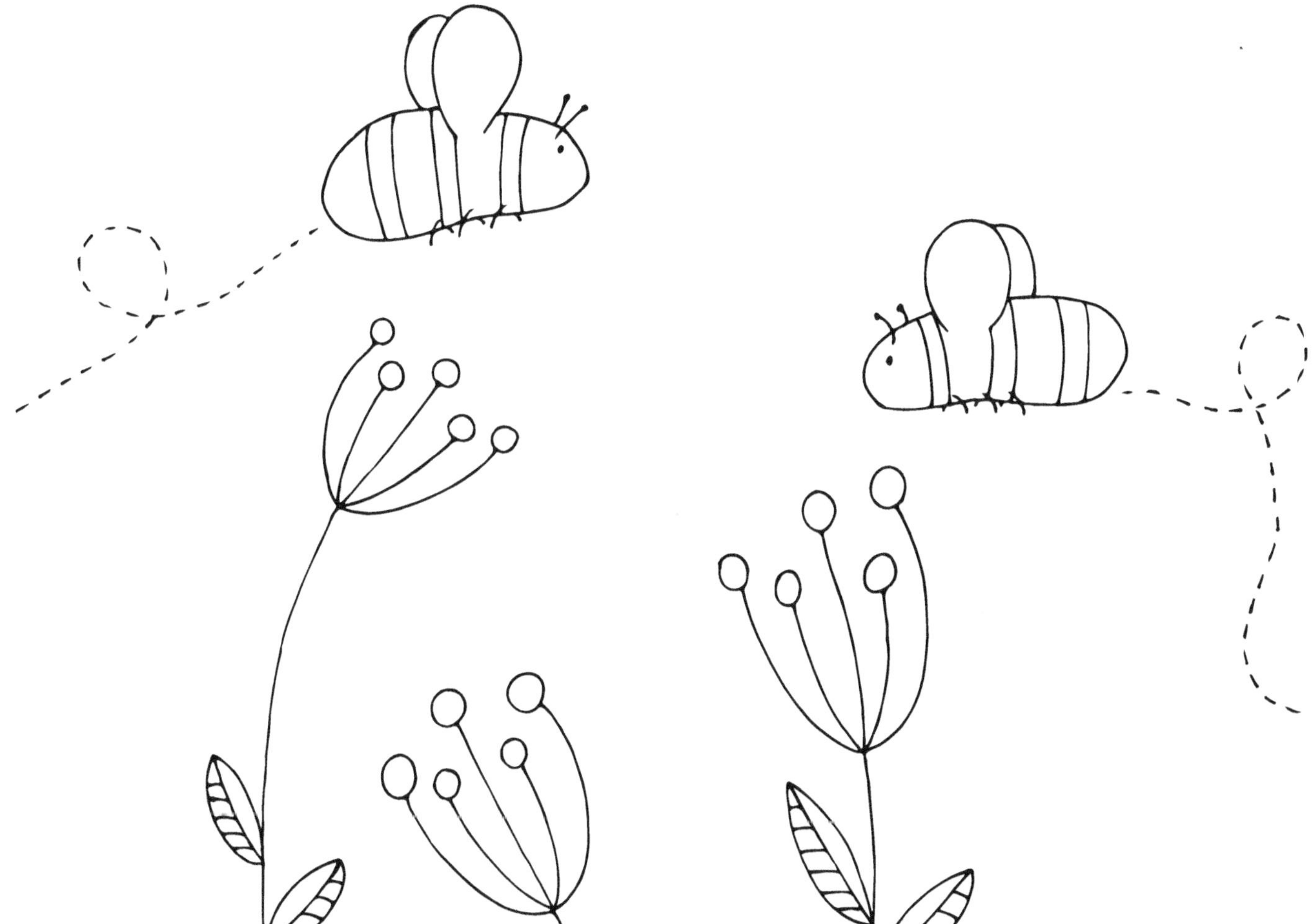

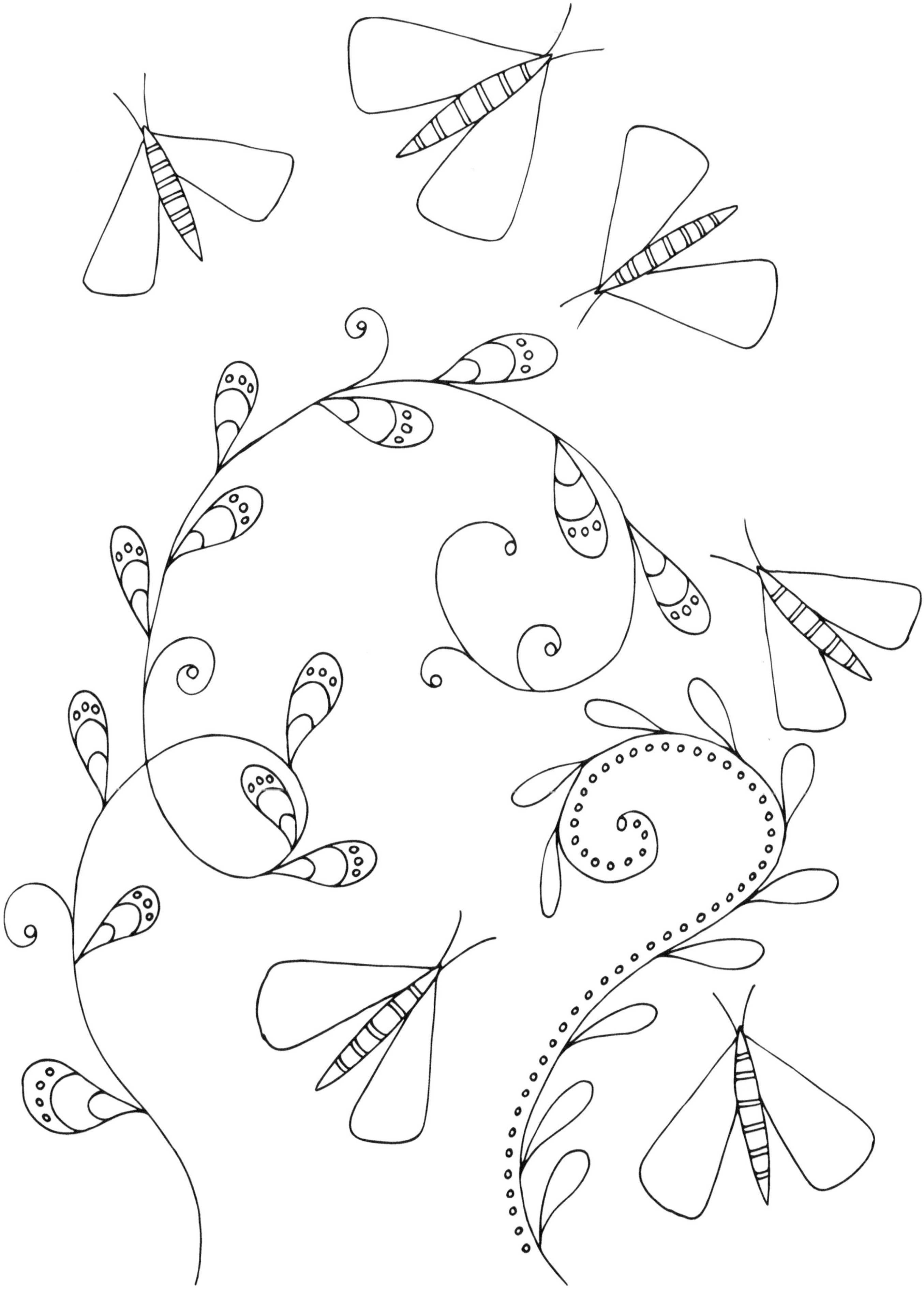

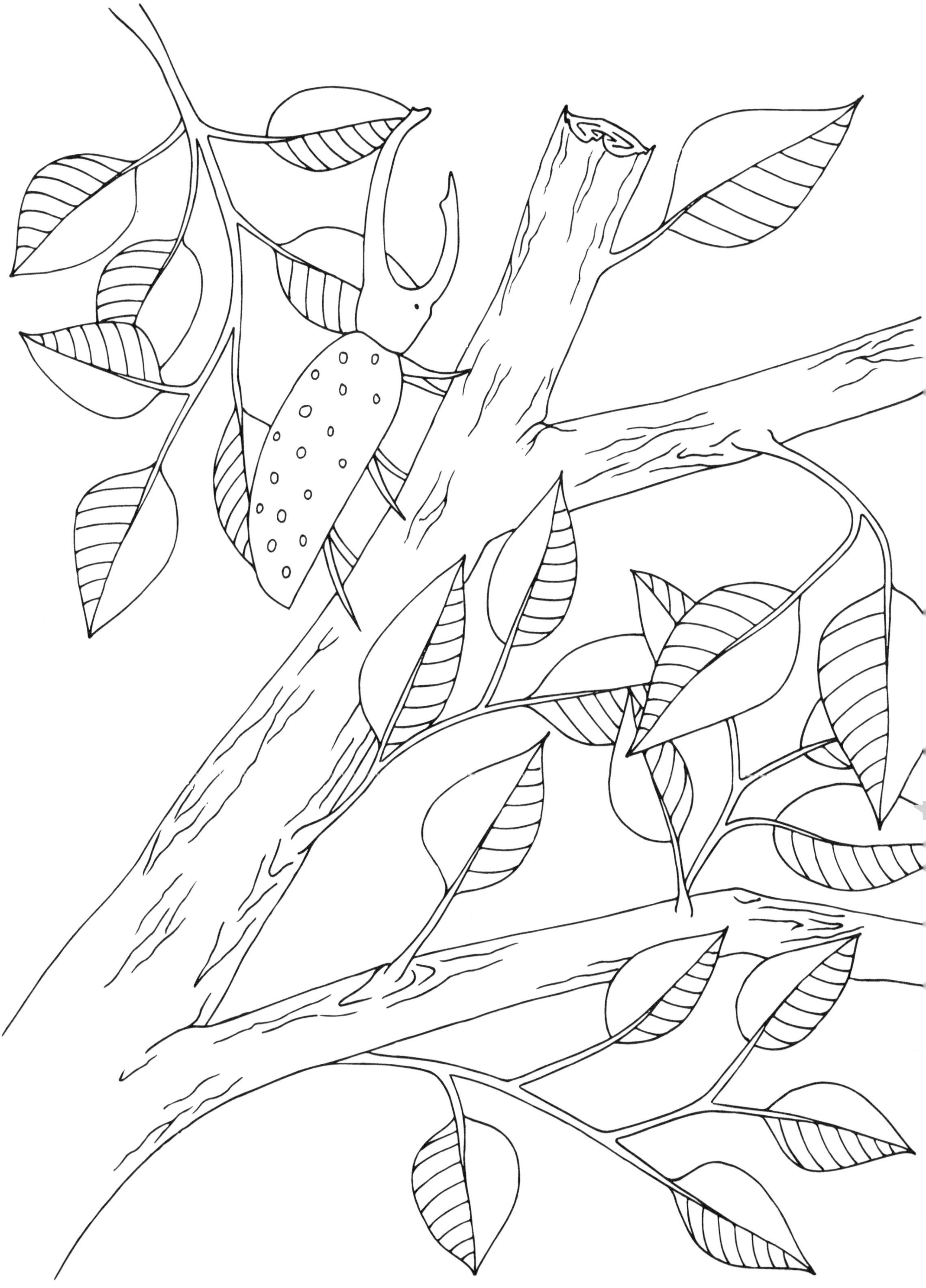

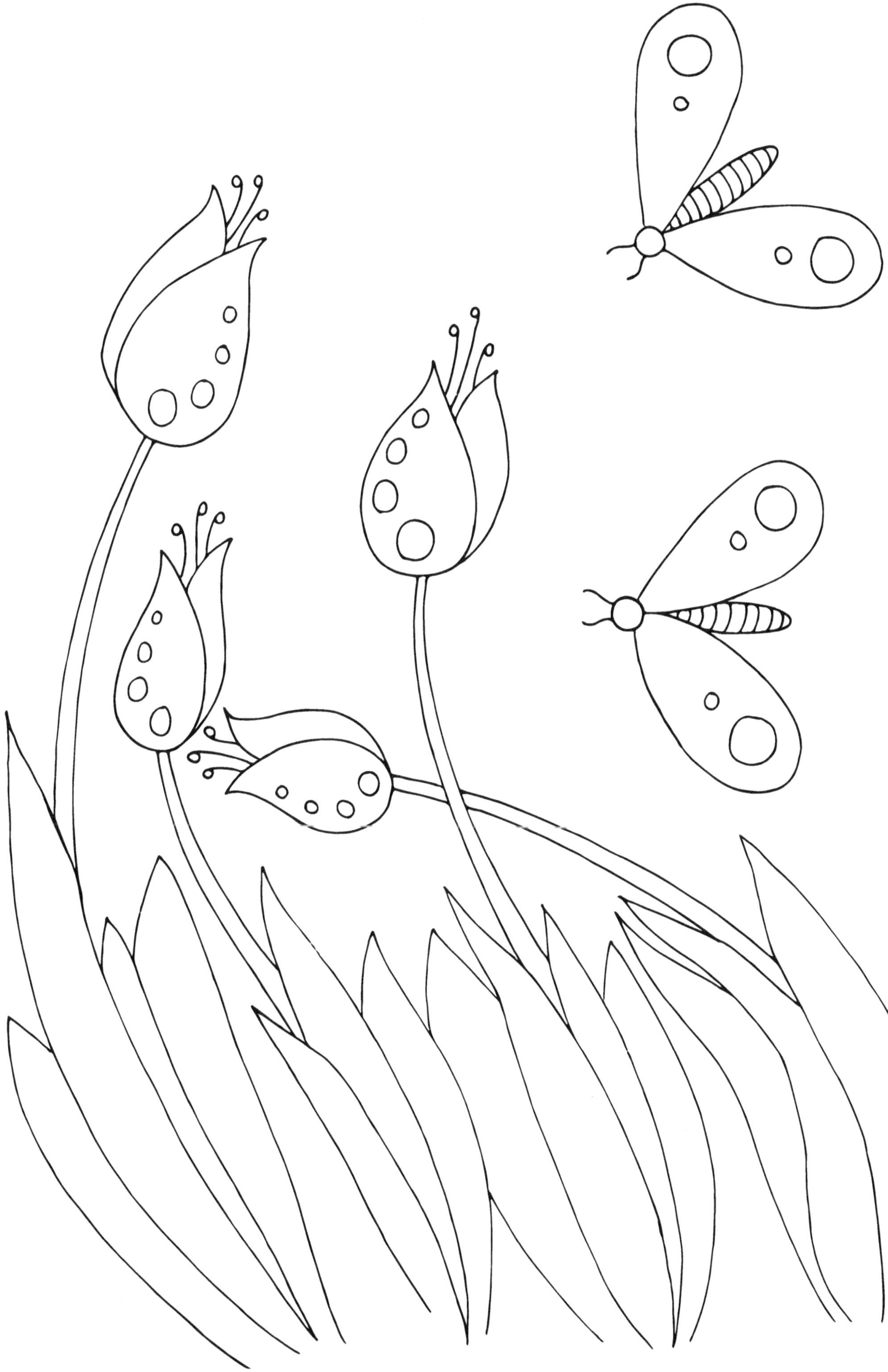

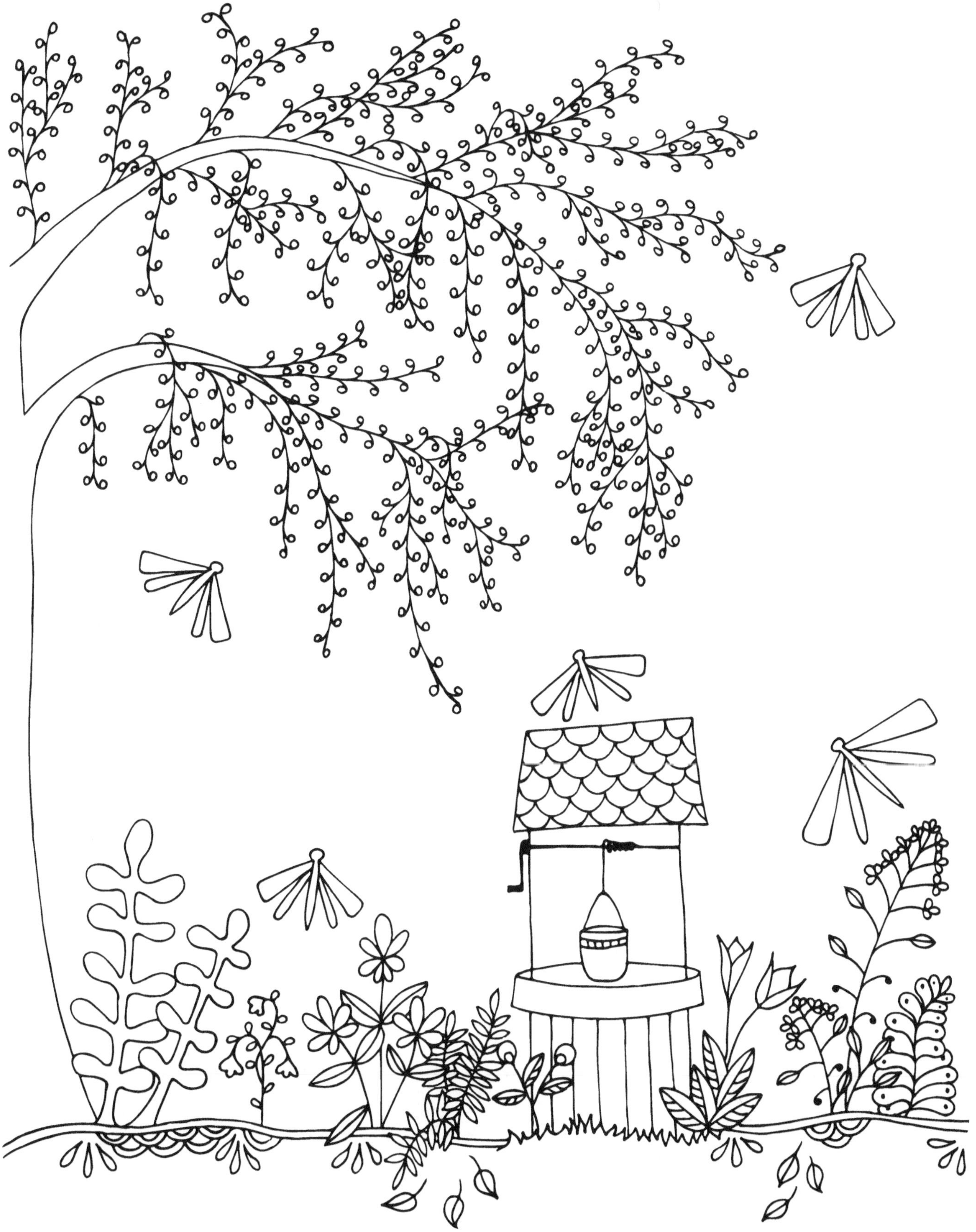

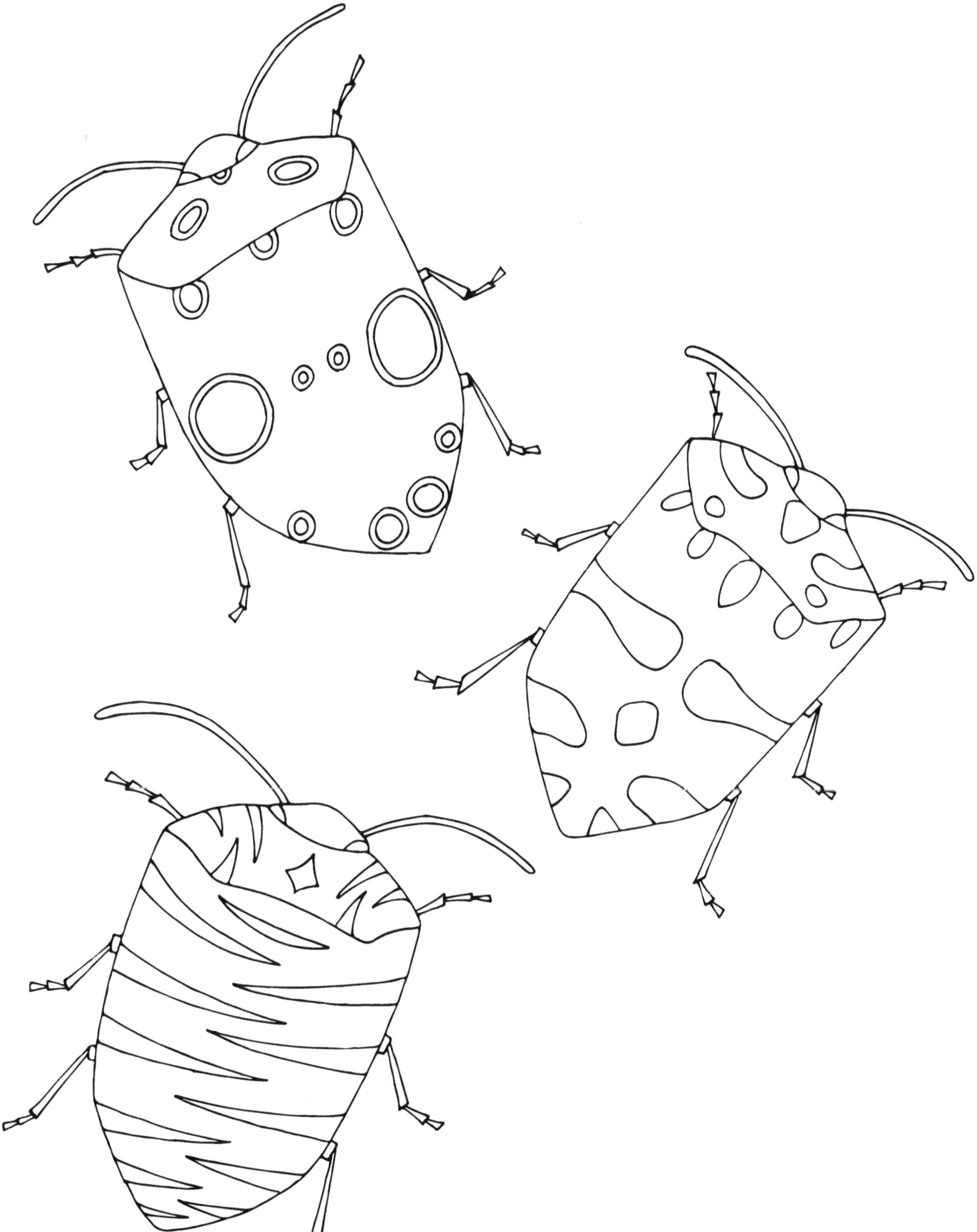

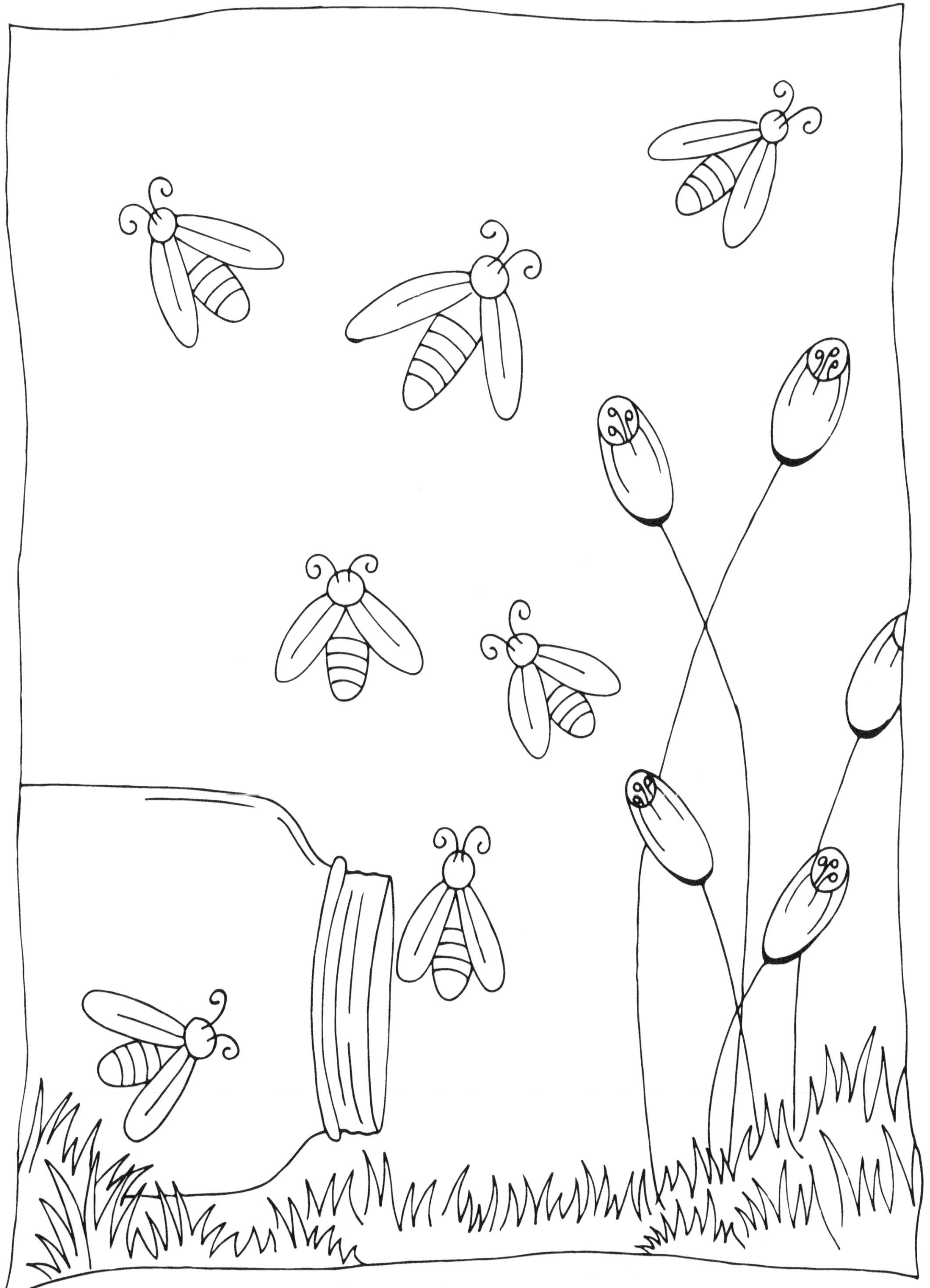

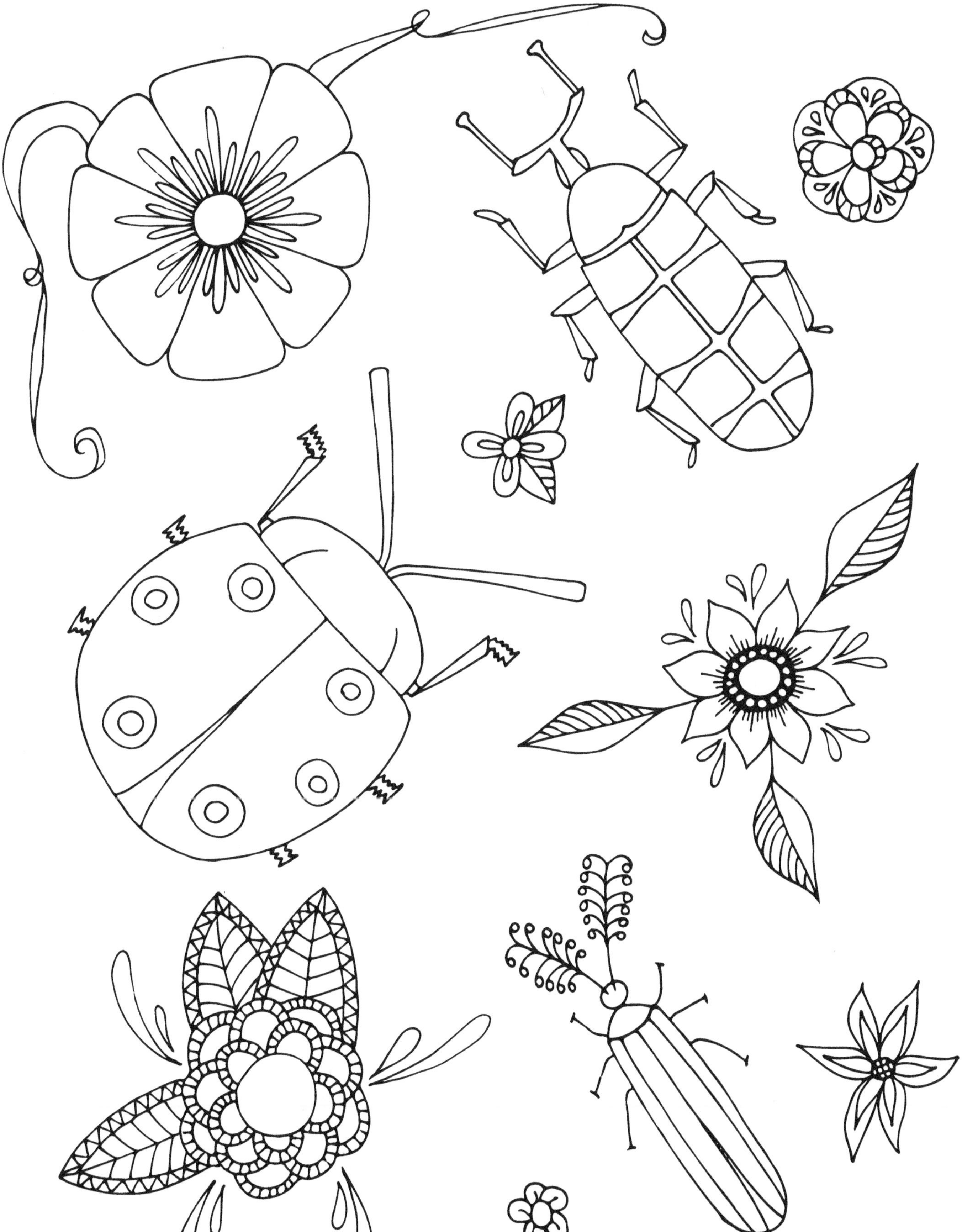

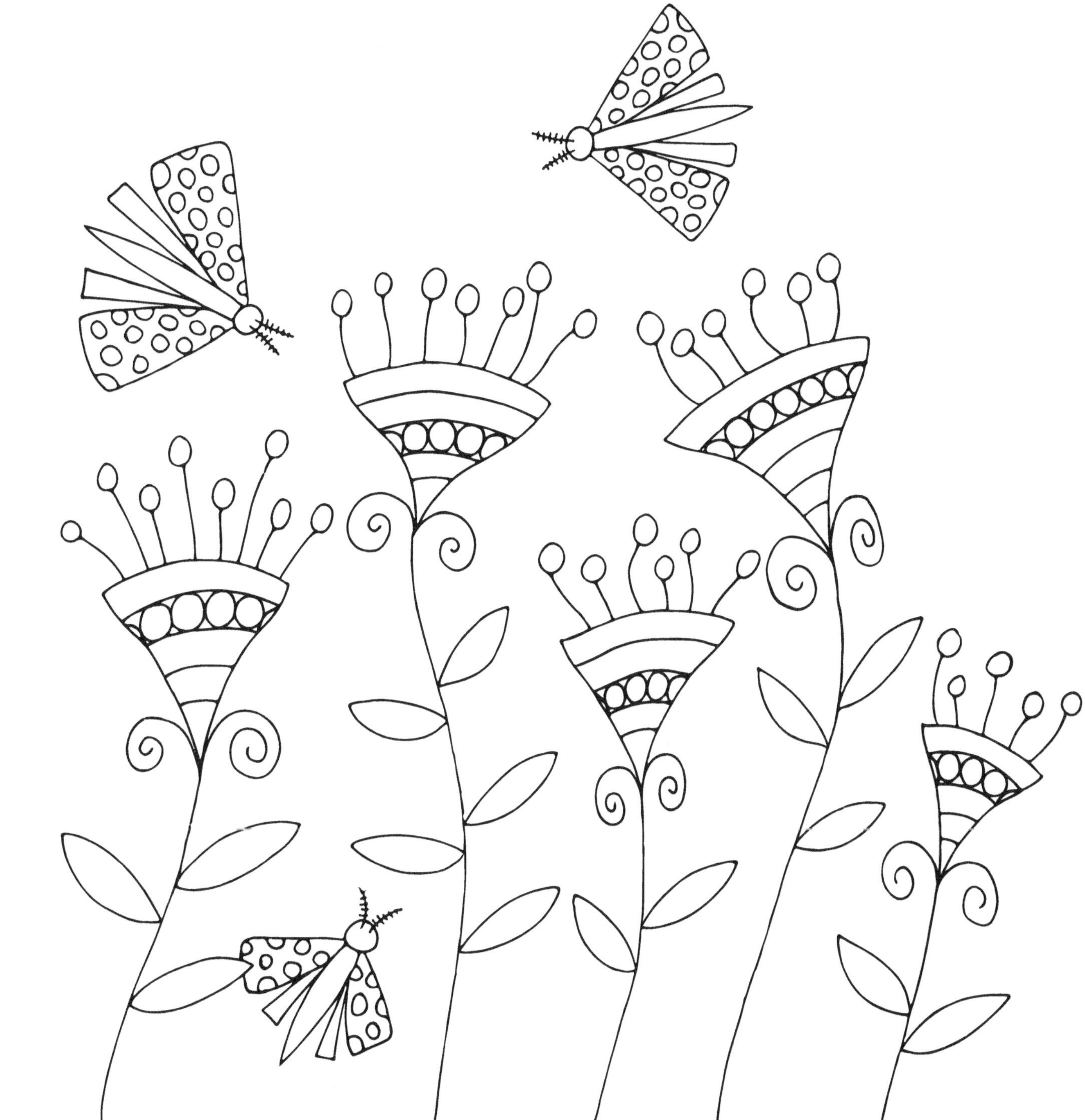

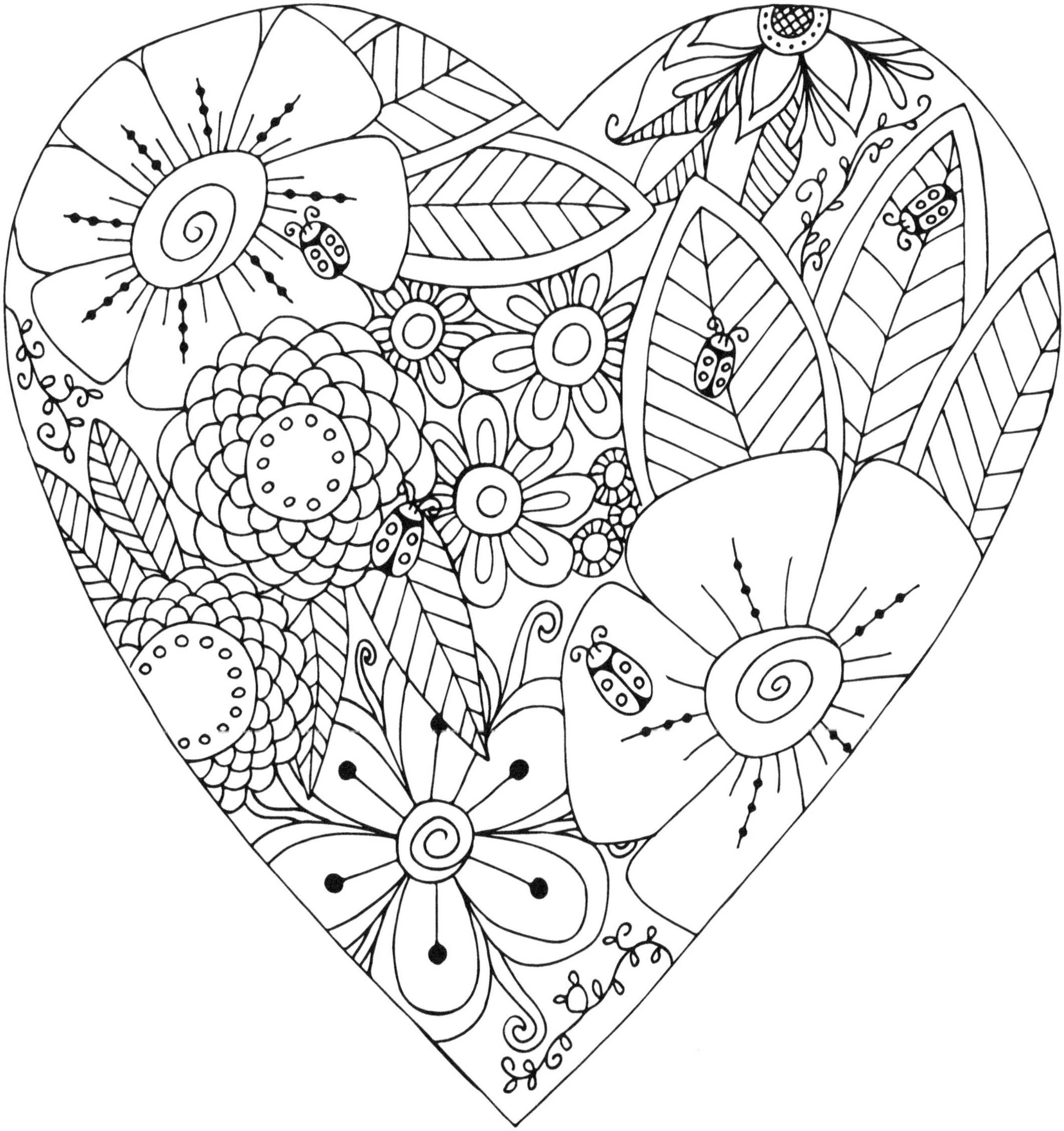

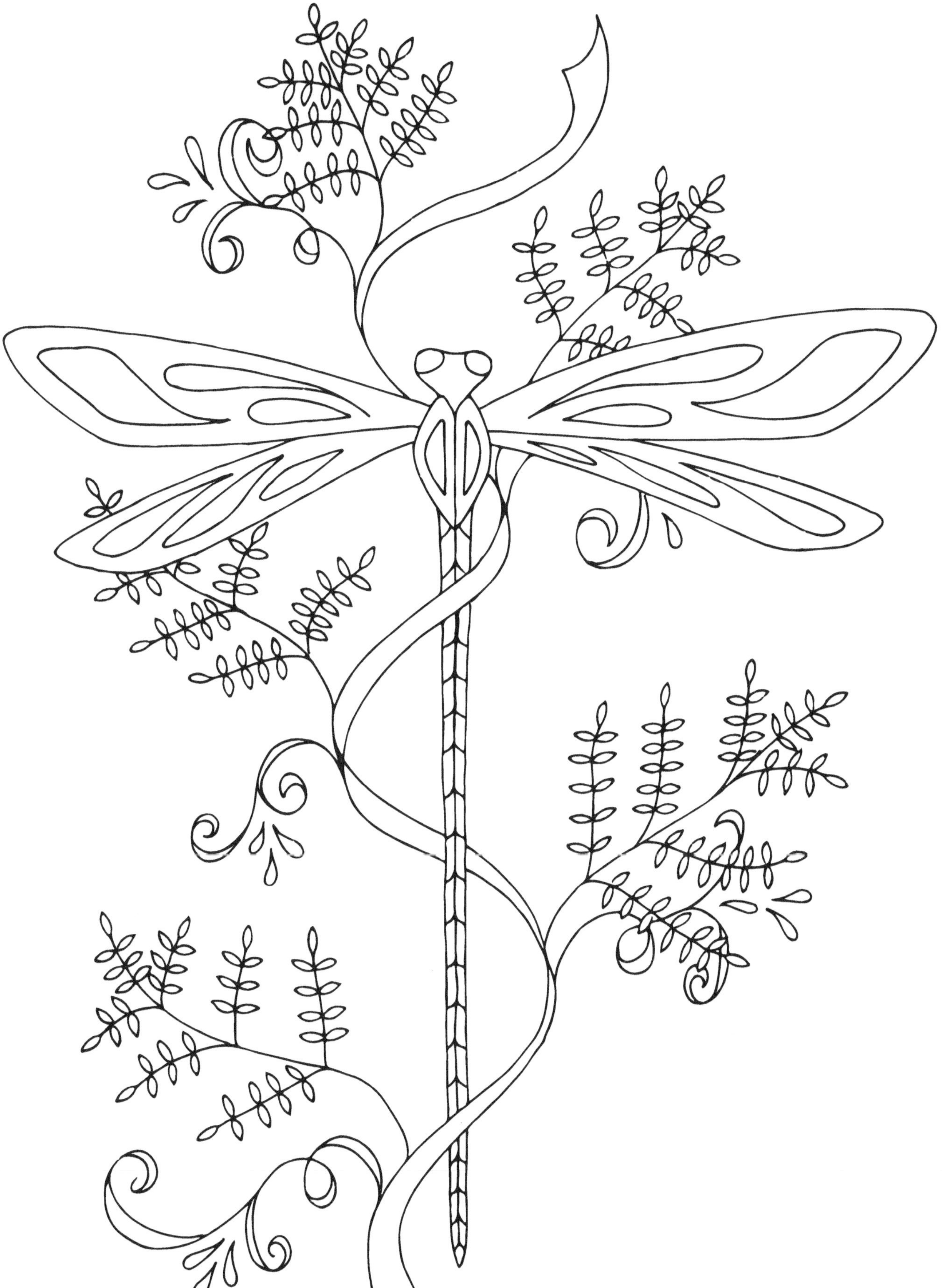

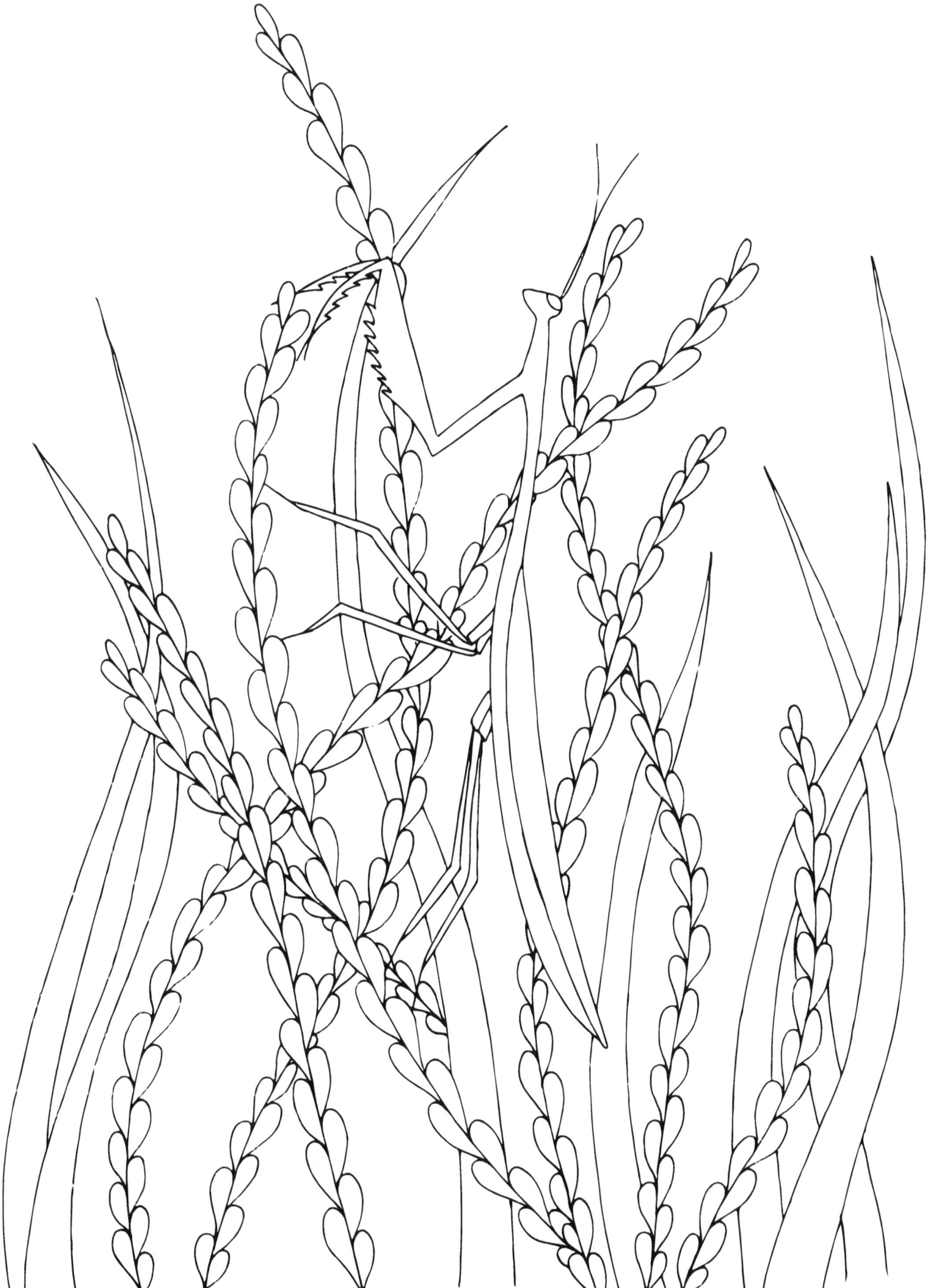

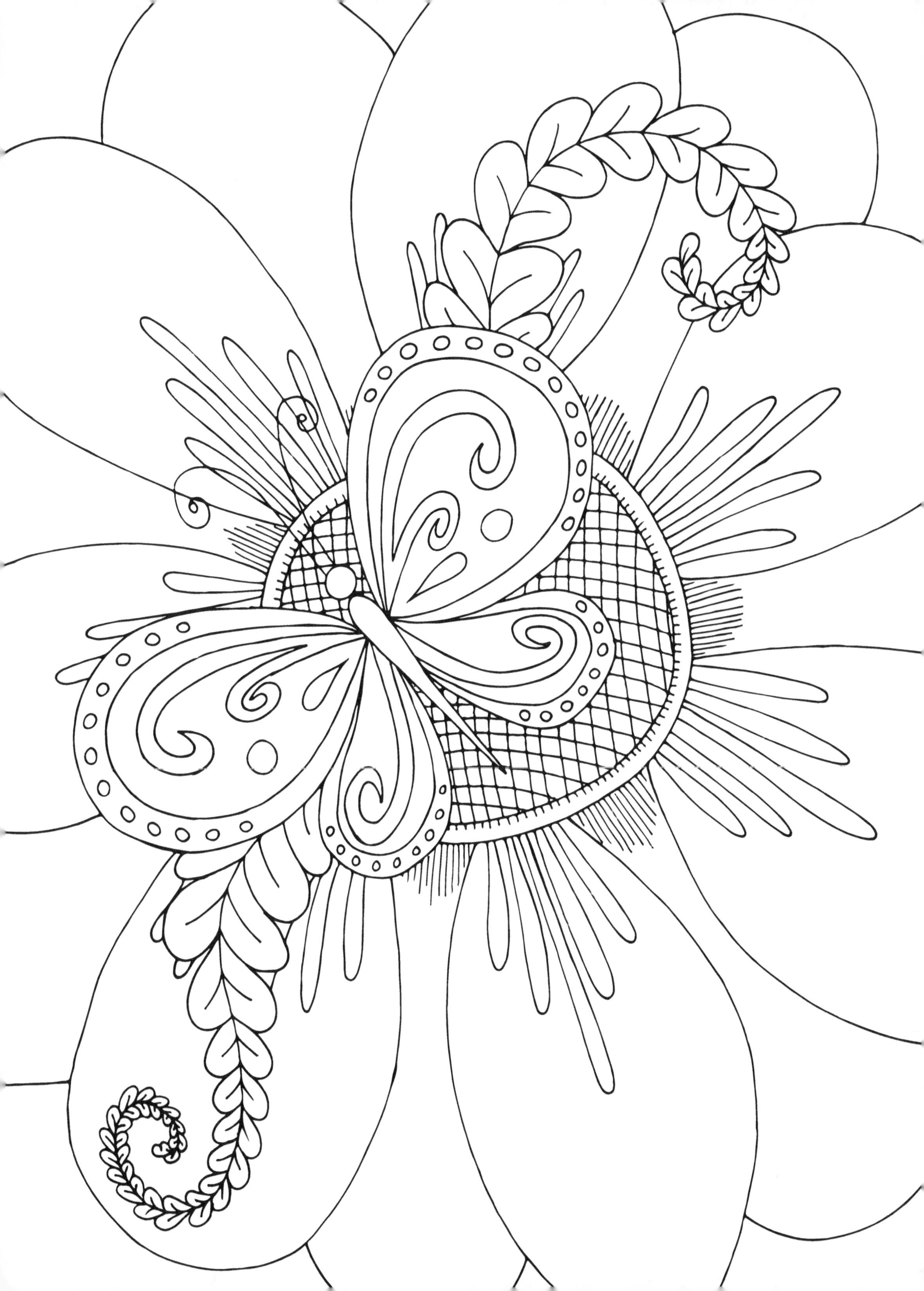

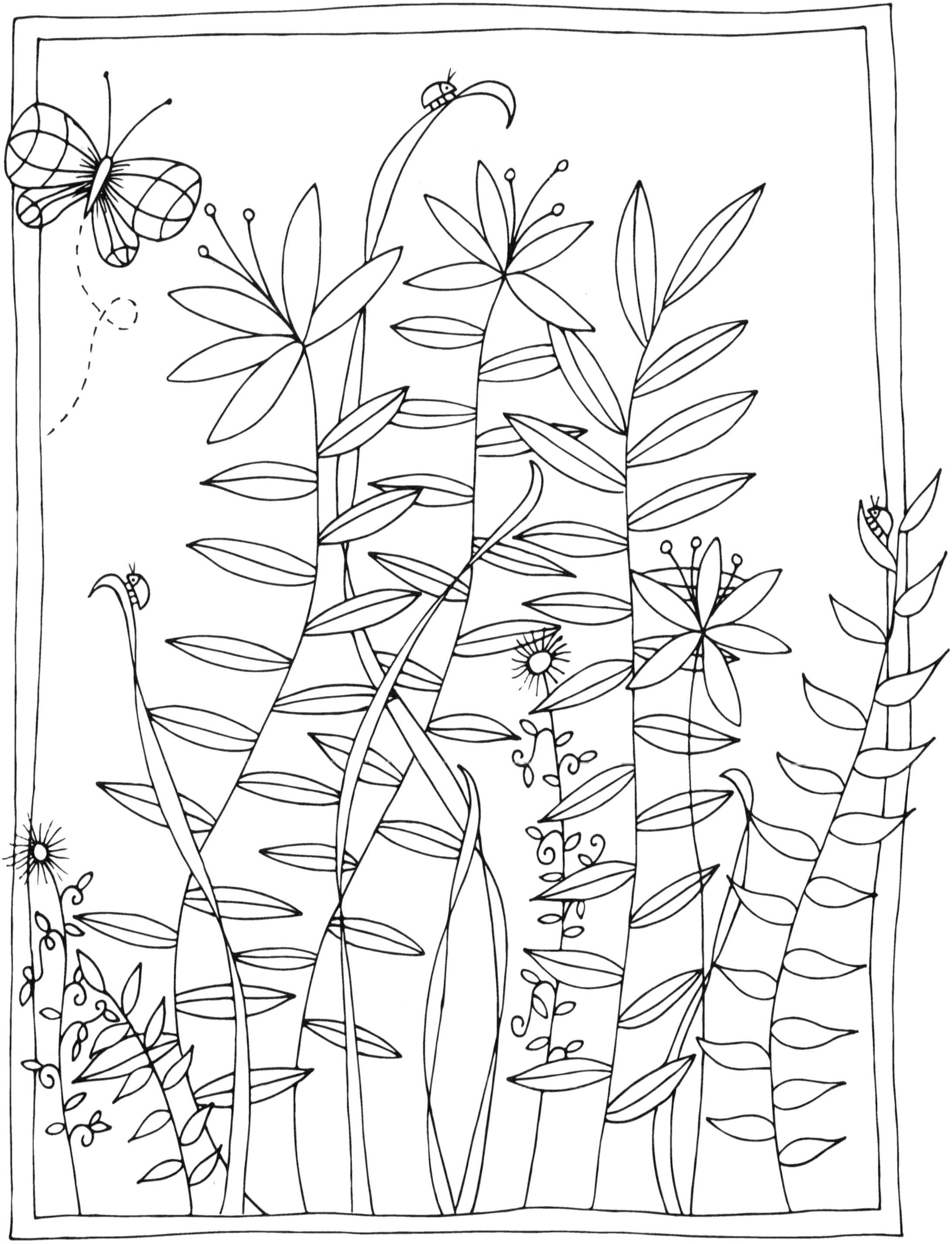

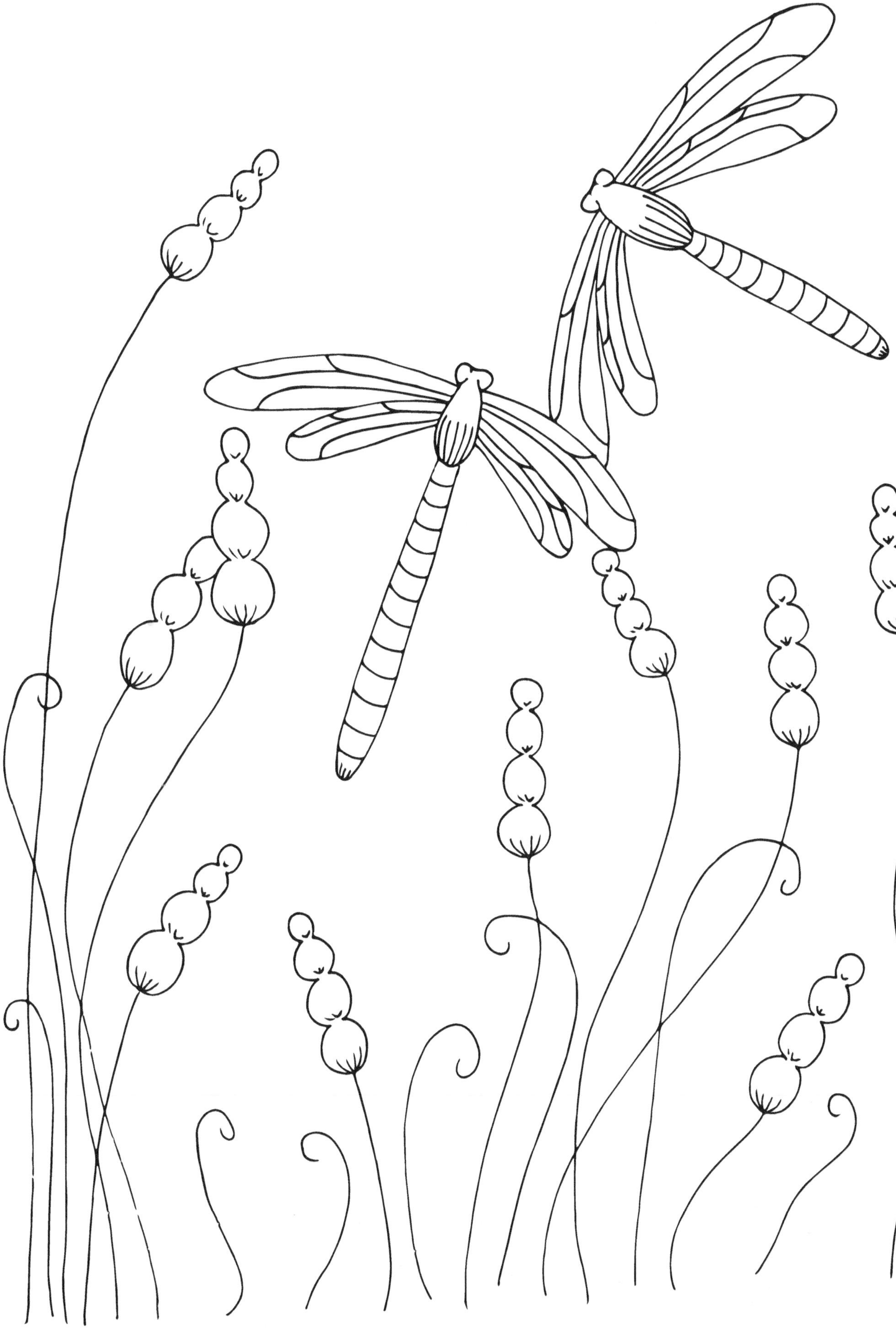

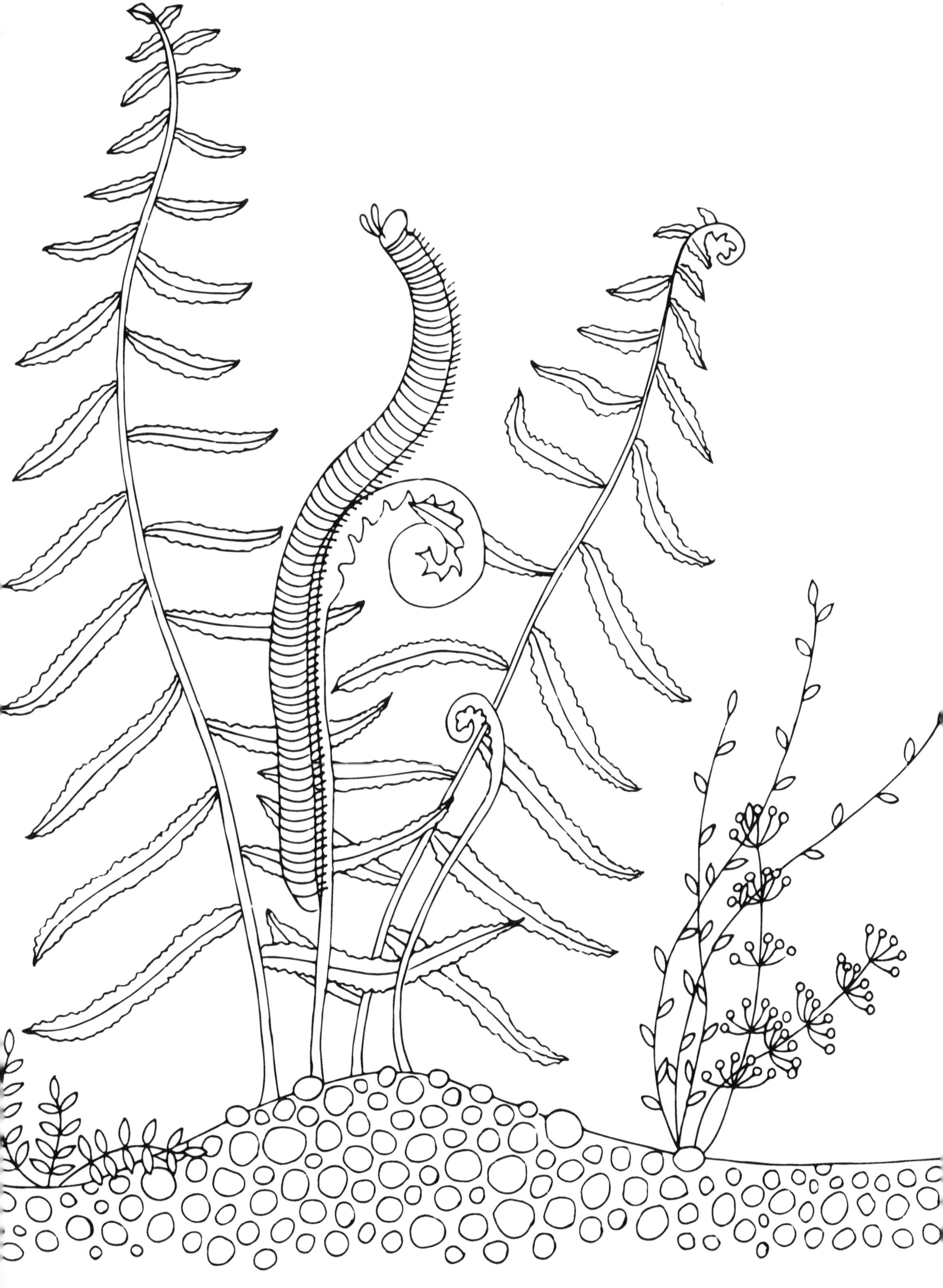

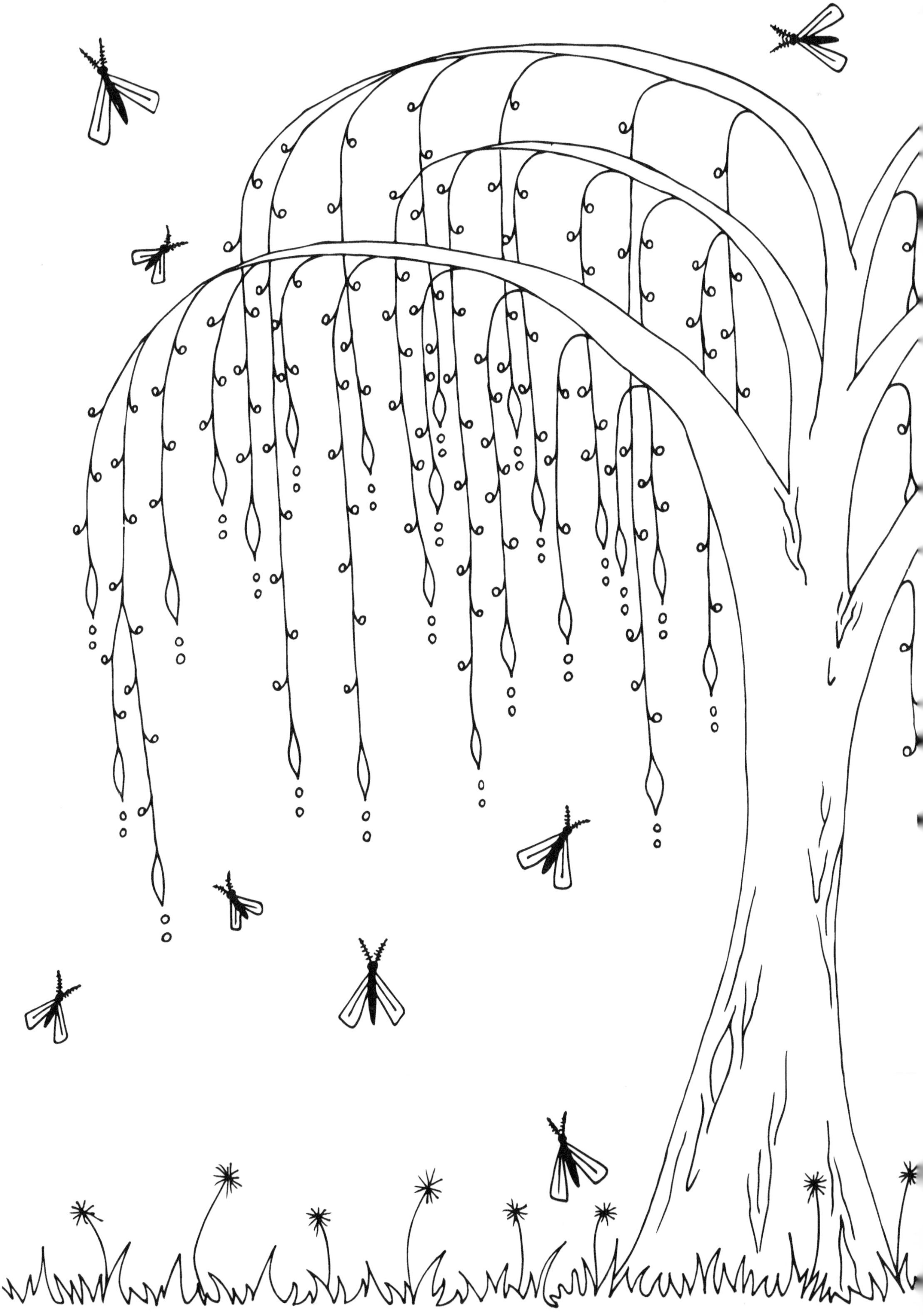

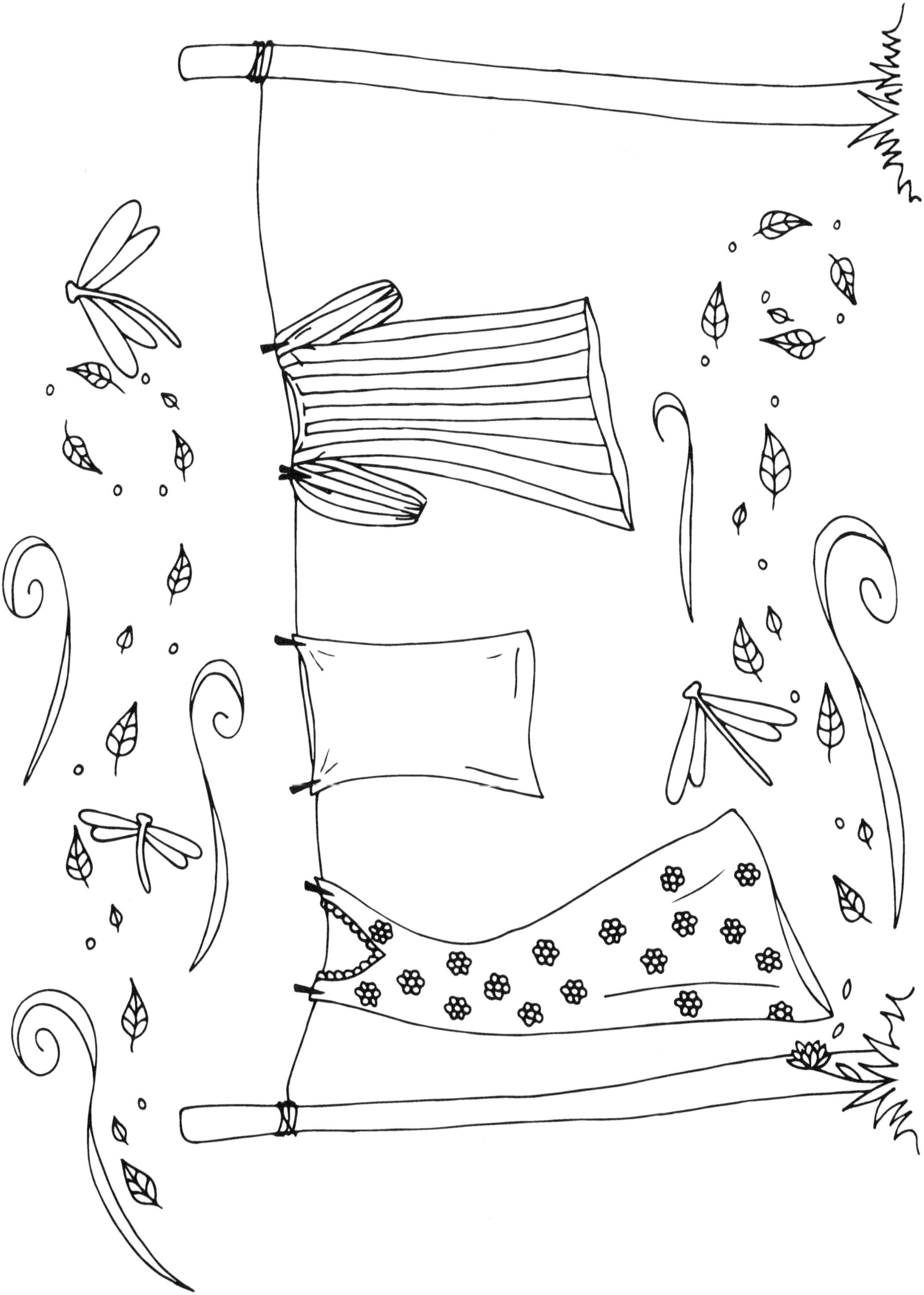

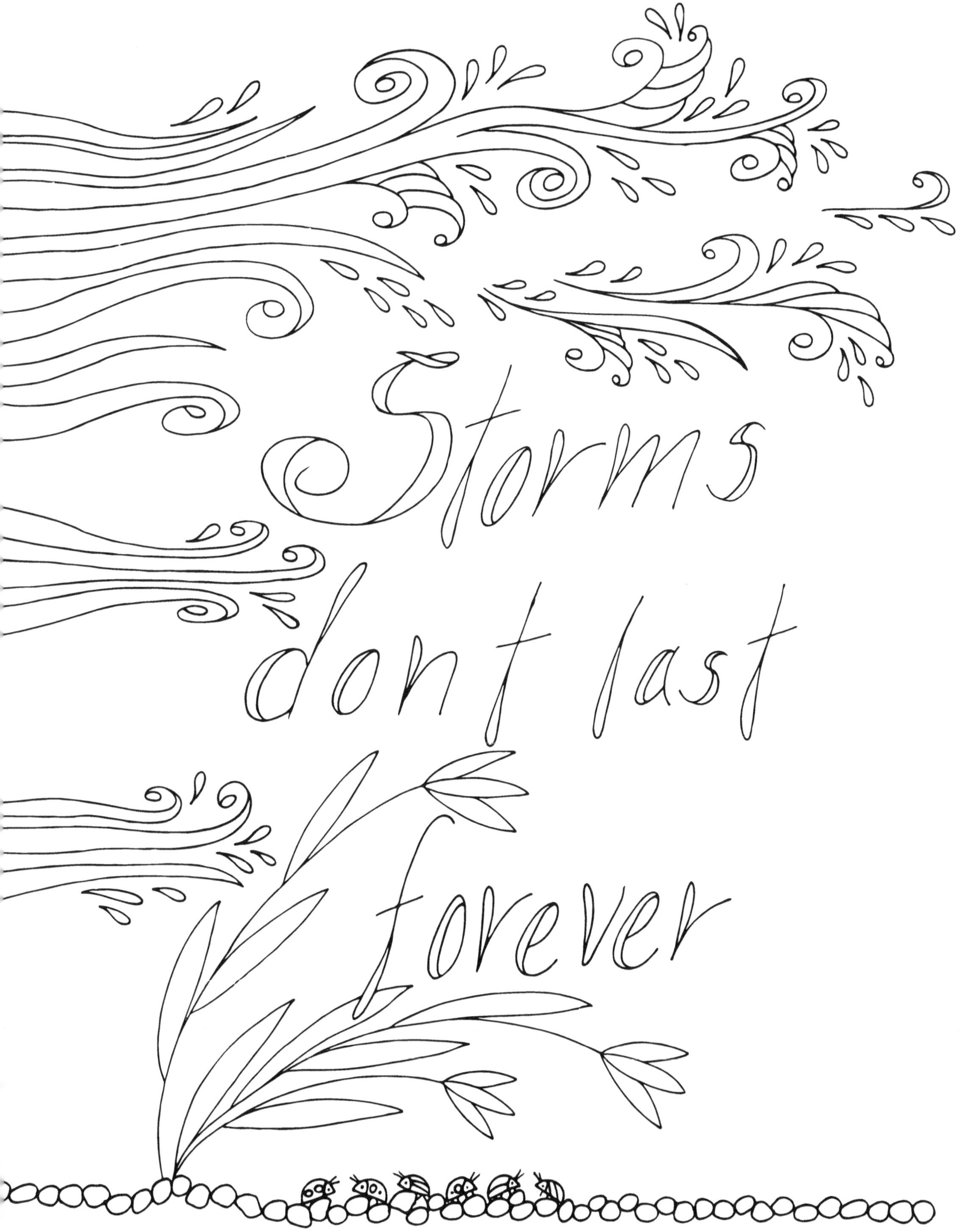
Storms
dont last
forever

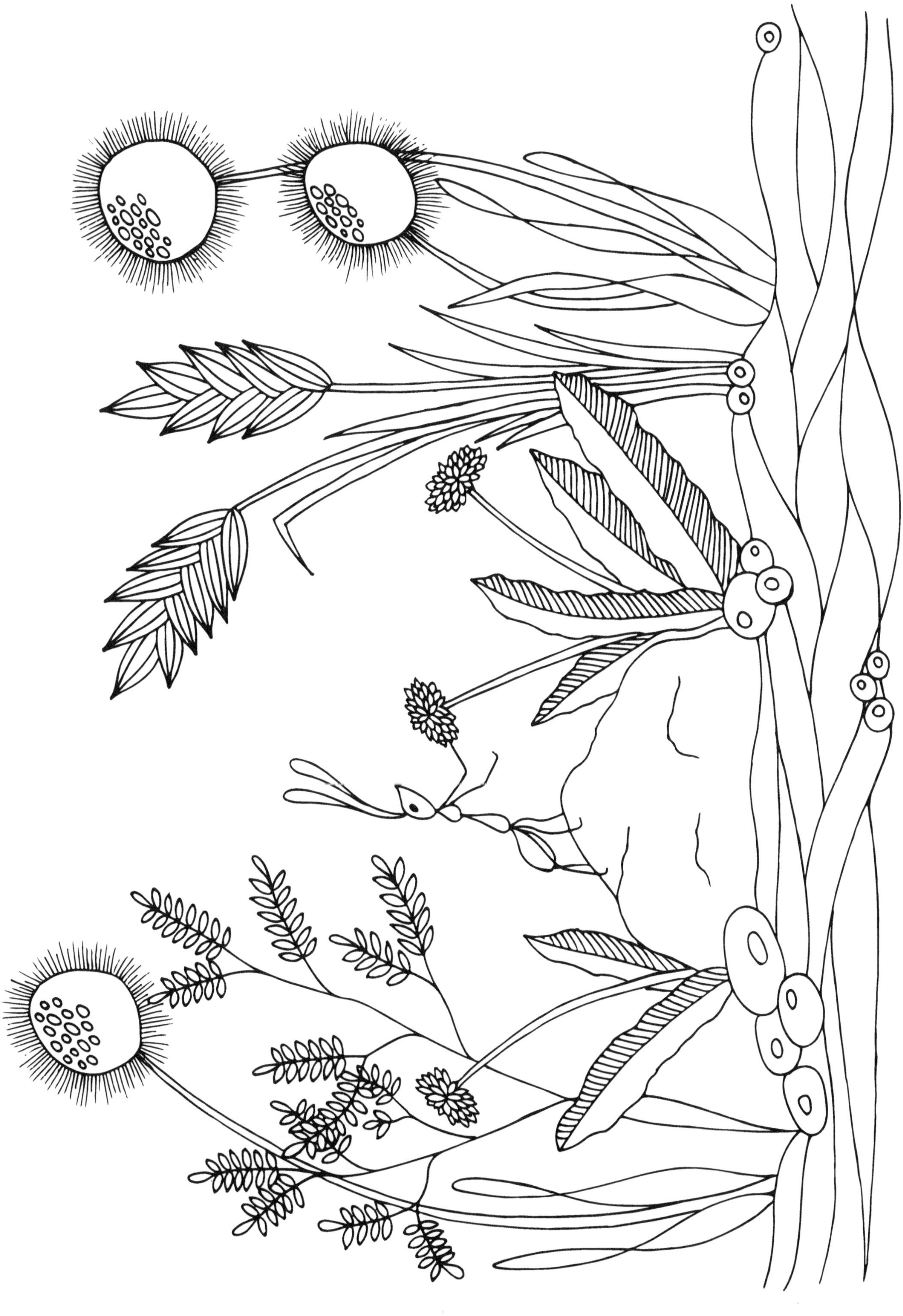

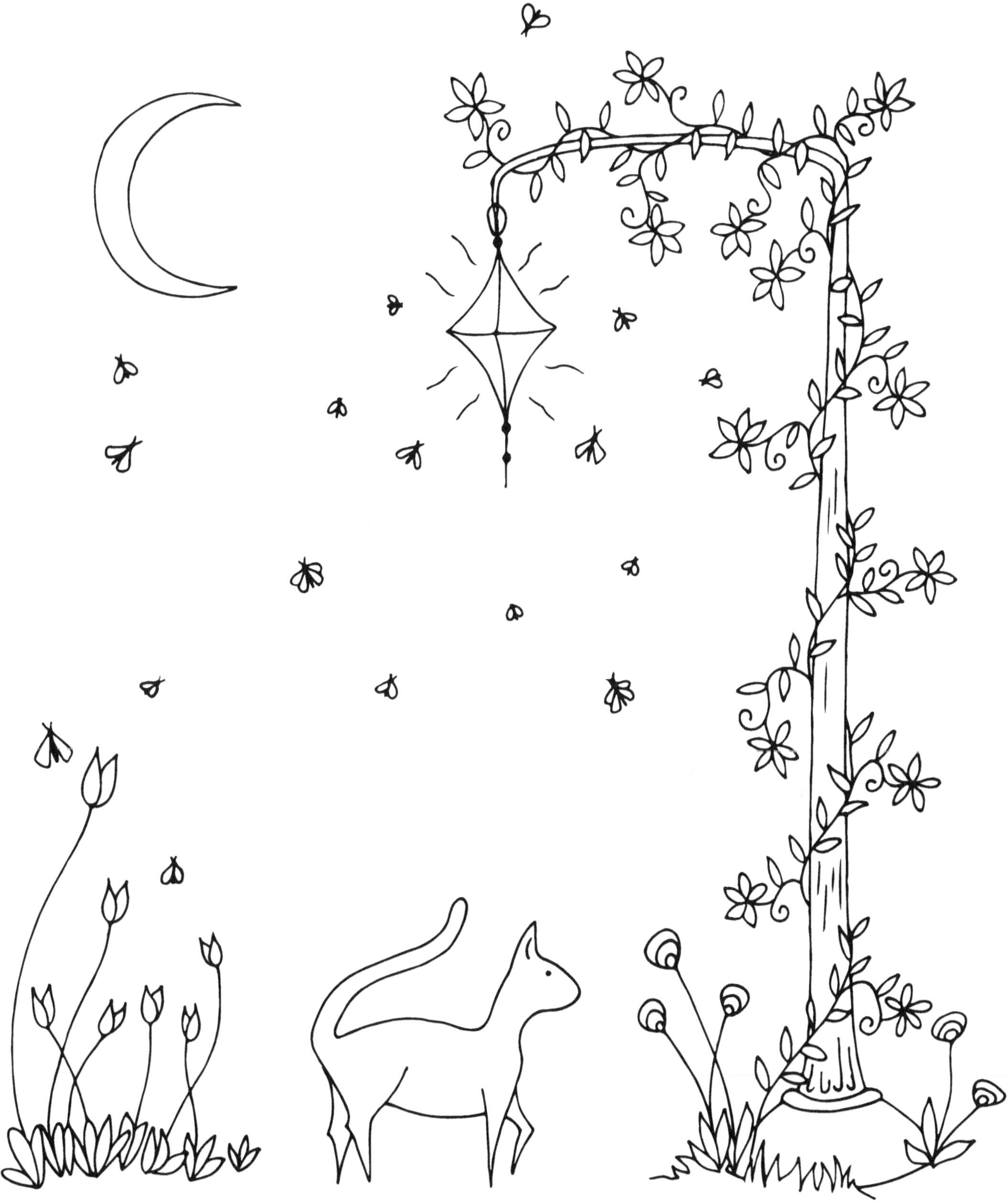

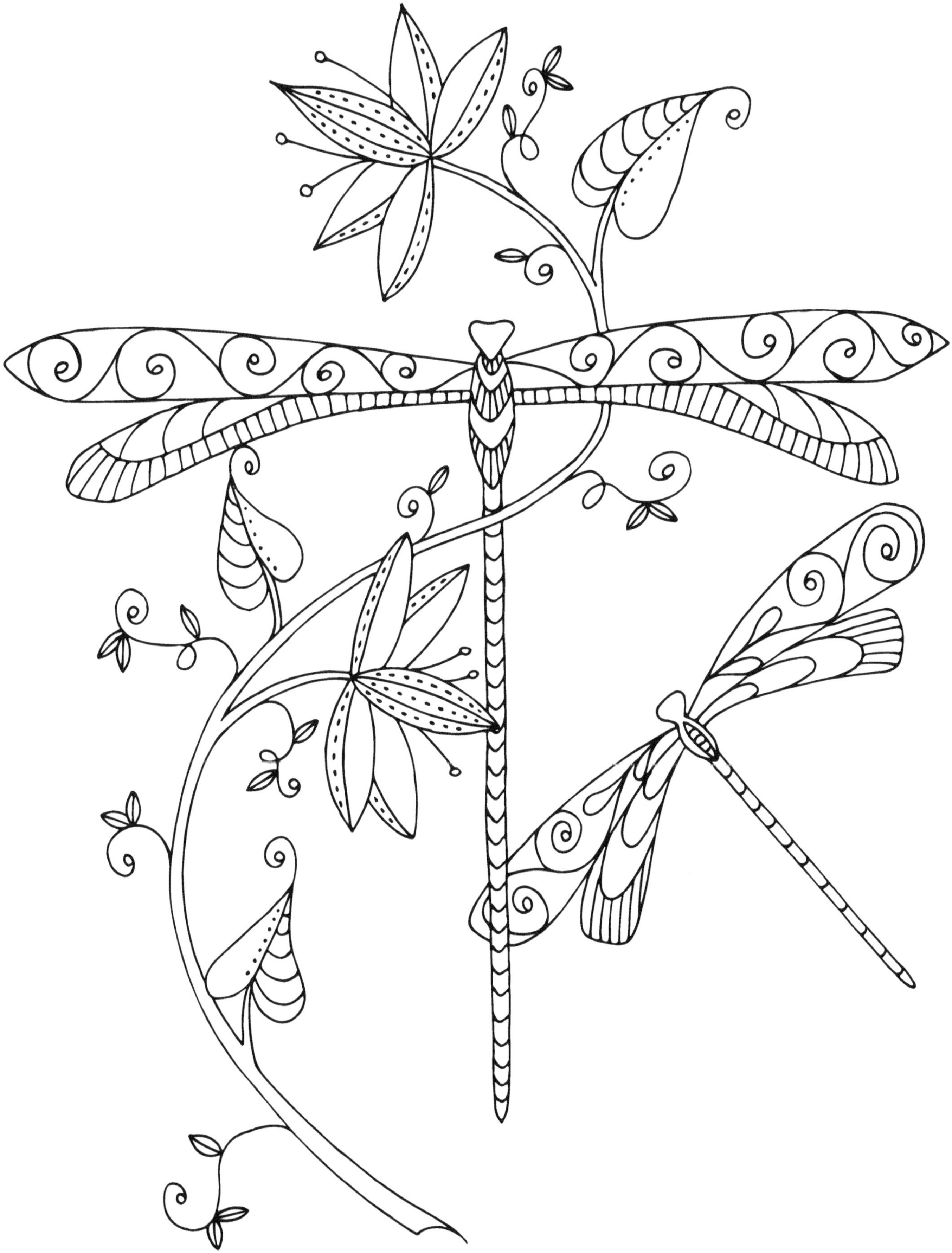

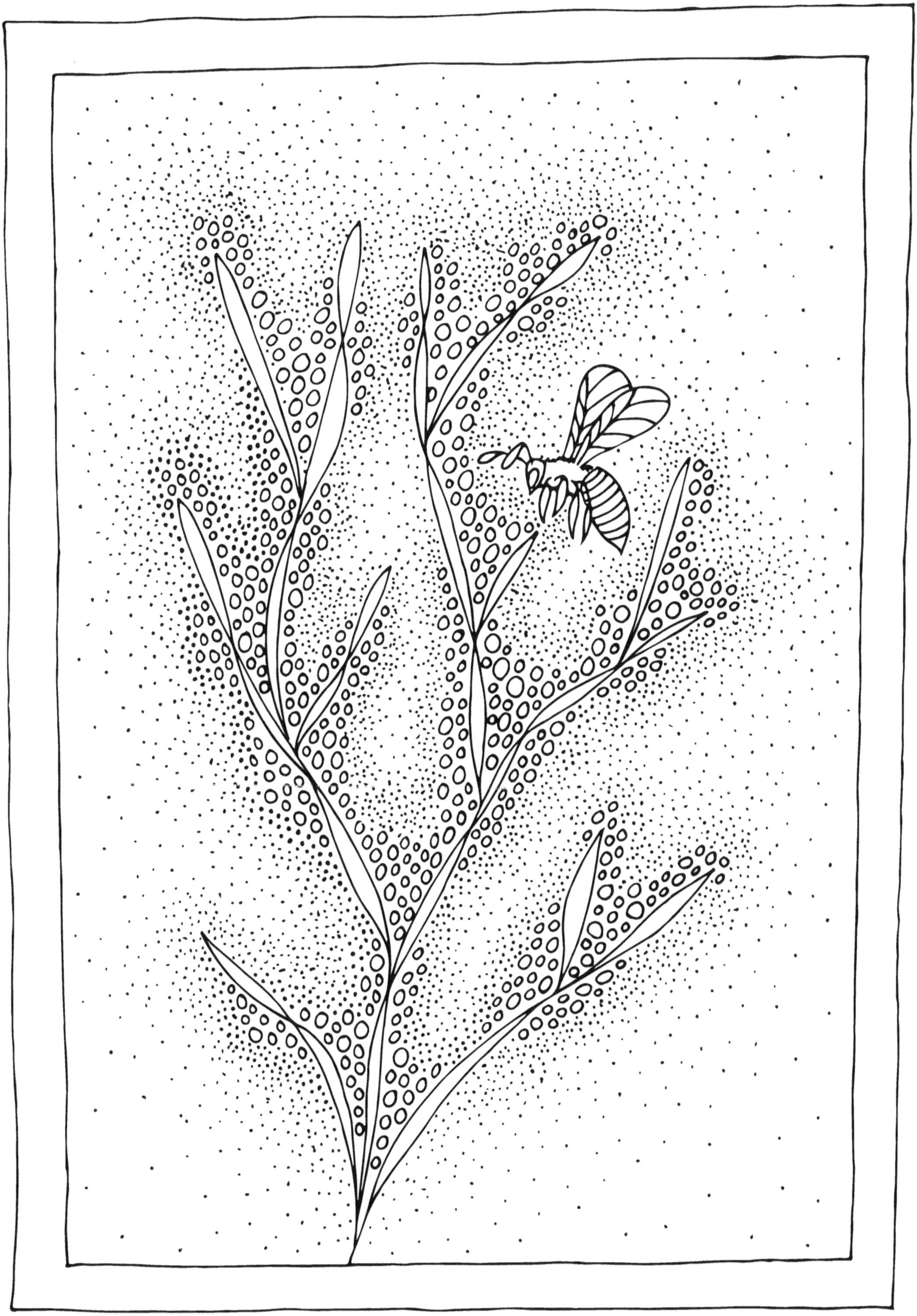

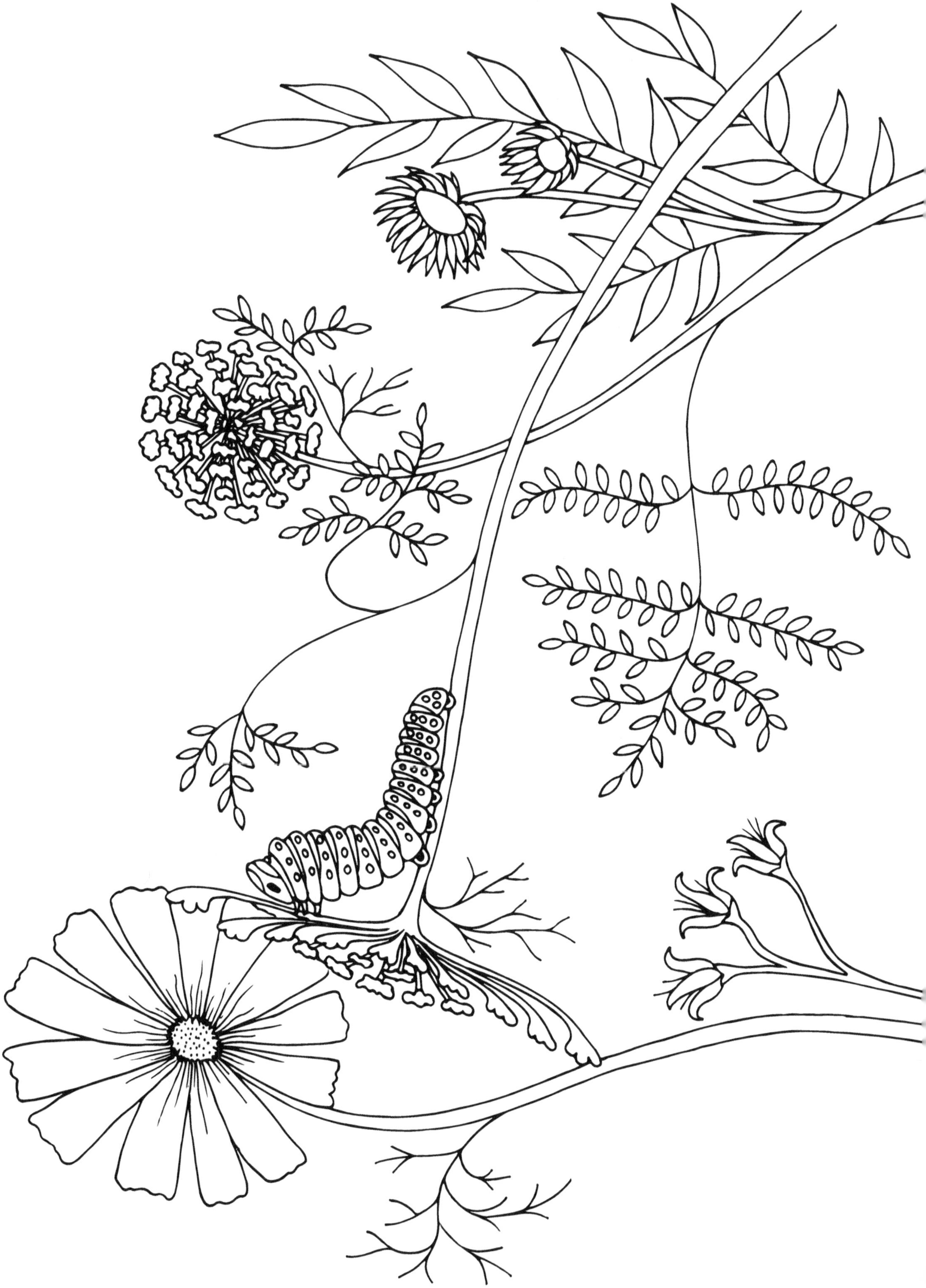

www.ingramcontent.com/pod-product-compliance
Lightning Source LLC
Chambersburg PA
CBHW080630190526
45169CB00009B/3350